J. K. M. Auchinleck

2 Castle Street

CRAIL.

THE GREEN PASTURES

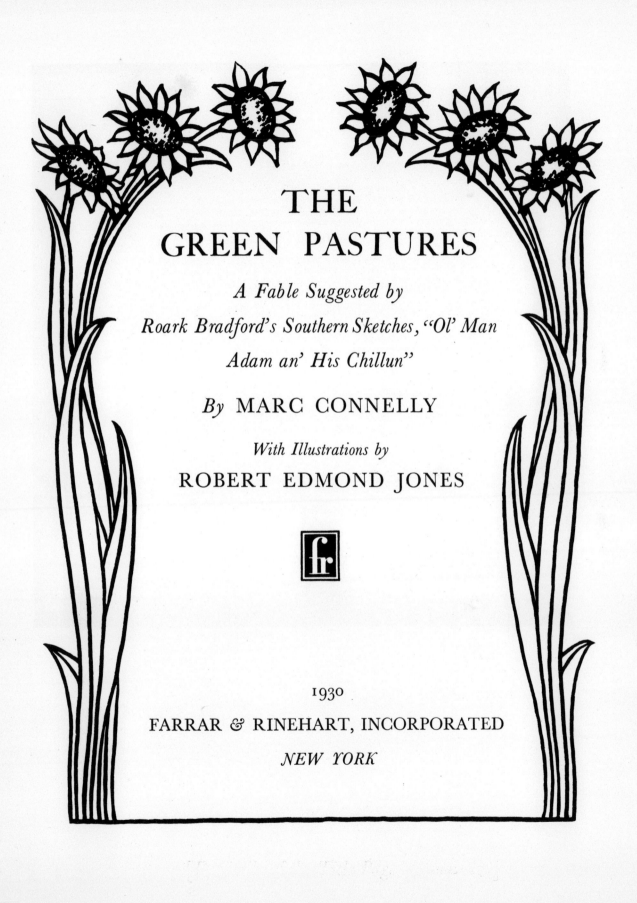

THE
GREEN PASTURES

A Fable Suggested by
Roark Bradford's Southern Sketches, "Ol' Man
Adam an' His Chillun"

By MARC CONNELLY

With Illustrations by
ROBERT EDMOND JONES

1930
FARRAR & RINEHART, INCORPORATED
NEW YORK

COPYRIGHT, 1930,

BY MARC CONNELLY

PRINTED IN THE UNITED STATES

OF AMERICA

BY THE LAKESIDE PRESS

CHICAGO

TO
ROWLAND STEBBINS

FOREWORD

IT WILL *be obvious to anyone who inspects this book that it is less a handsome edition of "The Green Pastures" with illustrations by Robert Edmond Jones than it is a collection of Robert Edmond Jones' drawings accompanied by the text of the play. It is a happy experience for the author to find his work in such magnificent company. But it is not a novelty. It was Mr. Jones whose enormously sympathetic imagination fashioned the scenery and costumes for the play's production, and realized, despite innumerable technical difficulties, a closer homogeneity with the text than I can recall ever having observed in the theatre.*

This happy consonance was partly due to a common approach to the play by Mr. Jones as designer and myself as director. I found it necessary that the actors have a perspective on their unfamiliar work as participants in a miracle play. This perspective was attained by suggesting that they regard themselves as members of a church in a small Southern town, and the play as something written by one of them for a local performance.

Mr. Jones' fancy transported him to the same small town where he became a leader in church activities. He borrowed what scenery the manager of the local opera house would lend; the cut wood wings, the foliage borders, etc. Then thrown back on his own resources, he designed simple two-dimensional settings with which to indicate Heaven, the Garden of Eden and other back-

ix

grounds in the play. Some of the costumes were also borrowed by Deacon Jones. The ermine cloak of the King of Babylon had originally proclaimed the regality of another king at a Mardi Gras. A neighbor loaned a Confederate uniform which would give a military touch to the scene in Pharaoh's court. Costumes for a fireman and a Scotchman, also happily available, were placed in the same scene because they agreed so pleasantly with the red cloaks of the courtiers. Of course the majority of the more elaborate costumes were made by the ladies of the congregation from designs the Deacon gave them. As a result, when the now well-oriented actors came to the dress rehearsal they found their garments and the scenery exactly those which an artistic fellow-member of the church might have been expected to provide. And as Deacon Jones was also Robert Edmond Jones they all had great beauty.

MARC CONNELLY

THE *following is a copy of the program of the first performance of "The Green Pastures," as presented at the Mansfield Theatre, New York City, Wednesday evening, February 26th, 1930:*

LAURENCE RIVERS INC. *Presents*

THE GREEN PASTURES

A FABLE

By MARC CONNELLY

SETTINGS BY ROBERT EDMOND JONES
MUSIC UNDER THE DIRECTION OF HALL JOHNSON
PLAY STAGED BY THE AUTHOR

"The Green Pastures" was suggested by Roark Bradford's Southern Sketches, "Ol' Man Adam an' His Chillun"

CAST OF CHARACTERS
(In the order of their appearance)

MR. DESHEE	Charles H. Moore
MYRTLE	Alicia Escamilla
FIRST BOY	Jazzlips Richardson, Jr.
SECOND BOY	Howard Washington
THIRD BOY	Reginald Blythwood
RANDOLPH	Joe Byrd
A COOK	Frances Smith
CUSTARD MAKER	Homer Tutt
FIRST MAMMY ANGEL	Anna Mae Fritz
A STOUT ANGEL	Josephine Byrd
A SLENDER ANGEL	Edna Thrower
ARCHANGEL	J. A. Shipp
GABRIEL	Wesley Hill
THE LORD	Richard B. Harrison

CHOIR LEADER	McKinley Reeves
ADAM	Daniel L. Haynes
EVE	Inez Richardson Wilson
CAIN	Lou Vernon
CAIN'S GIRL	Dorothy Randolph
ZEBA	Edna M. Harris
CAIN THE SIXTH	James Fuller
BOY GAMBLER	Louis Kelsey
FIRST GAMBLER	Collington Hayes
SECOND GAMBLER	Ivan Sharp
VOICE IN SHANTY	Josephine Byrd
NOAH	Tutt Whitney
NOAH'S WIFE	Susie Sutton
SHEM	Milton J. Williams
FIRST WOMAN	Dinks Thomas
SECOND WOMAN	Anna Mae Fritz
THIRD WOMAN	Geneva Blythwood
FIRST MAN	Emory Richardson
FLATFOOT	Freddie Archibald
HAM	Homer Tutt
JAPHETH	Stanleigh Morrell
FIRST CLEANER	Josephine Byrd
SECOND CLEANER	Florence Fields
ABRAHAM	J. A. Shipp
ISAAC	Charles H. Moore
JACOB	Edgar Burks
MOSES	Alonzo Fenderson
ZIPPORAH	Mercedes Gilbert
AARON	McKinley Reeves
A CANDIDATE MAGICIAN	Reginald Fenderson
PHARAOH	George Randel
THE GENERAL	Walt McClane
FIRST WIZARD	Emory Richardson
HEAD MAGICIAN	Arthur Porter
JOSHUA	Stanleigh Morrell

xii

FIRST SCOUT	Ivan Sharp
MASTER OF CEREMONIES	·Billy Cumby
KING OF BABYLON	Jay Mondaaye
PROPHET	Ivan Sharp
HIGH PRIEST	Homer Tutt

THE KING'S FAVORITES . . . . . .
{
Leona Winkler
Florence Lee
Constance Van Dyke
Mary Ella Hart
Inez Persand
}

OFFICER	Emory Richardson
HEZDREL	Daniel L. Haynes
ANOTHER OFFICER	Stanleigh Morrell

THE CHILDREN

Philistine Bumgardner, Margery Bumgardner, Anthony Sylvester, Mary Sylvester, Fredia Longshaw, Wilbur Cohen, Jr., Verdon Perdue, Ruby Davis, Willmay Davis, Margerette Thrower, Viola Lewis

ANGELS AND TOWNSPEOPLE

Amy Escamilla, Elsie Byrd, Benveneta Washington, Thula Ortiz, Ruth Carl, Geneva Blythwood

BABYLONIAN BAND

Carl Shorter, Earl Bowie, Thomas Russell, Richard Henderson

THE CHOIR

Sopranos--Bertha Wright, Geraldine Gooding, Marie Warren, Mattie Harris, Elsie Thompson, Massie Patterson, Marguerite Avery

Altos—Evelyn Burwell, Ruthena Matson, Leona Avery, Mrs. Willie Mays, Viola Mickens, Charlotte Junius

Tenors—John Warren, Joe Loomis, Walter Hilliard, Harold Foster, Adolph Henderson, William McFarland, McKinley Reeves, Arthur Porter

Baritones—Marc D'Albert, Gerome Addison, Walter Whitfield, D. K. Williams

Bassos—Lester Holland, Cecil McNair, Tom Lee, Walter Meadows, Frank Horace

CHARACTERS

MR. DESHEE, THE PREACHER

MYRTLE

FIRST BOY

SECOND BOY

FIRST COOK

A VOICE

SECOND COOK

FIRST MAN ANGEL

FIRST MAMMY ANGEL

A STOUT ANGEL

A SLENDER ANGEL

ARCHANGEL

GABRIEL

GOD

CHOIR LEADER

CUSTARD MAKER

ADAM

EVE

CAIN

CAIN'S GIRL

ZEBA

CAIN THE SIXTH

BOY GAMBLER

FIRST GAMBLER

SECOND GAMBLER

VOICE IN SHANTY

NOAH

NOAH'S WIFE

SHEM

FIRST WOMAN

SECOND WOMAN

THIRD WOMAN

FIRST MAN

FLATFOOT

HAM

JAPHETH

FIRST CLEANER

SECOND CLEANER

ABRAHAM

ISAAC

JACOB

MOSES

ZIPPORAH

AARON

A CANDIDATE MAGICIAN

PHARAOH

GENERAL

HEAD MAGICIAN

FIRST WIZARD

SECOND WIZARD

JOSHUA

FIRST SCOUT

MASTER OF CEREMONIES

KING OF BABYLON

PROPHET

HIGH PRIEST

CORPORAL

HEZDREL

SECOND OFFICER

SCENES

PART I

I. THE SUNDAY SCHOOL

II. A FISH FRY

III. A GARDEN

IV. OUTSIDE THE GARDEN

V. A ROADSIDE

VI. A PRIVATE OFFICE

VII. ANOTHER ROADSIDE AND A HOUSE

VIII. A HOUSE

IX. A HILLSIDE

X. A MOUNTAIN TOP

PART II

I. THE PRIVATE OFFICE

II. THE MOUTH OF A CAVE

III. A THRONE ROOM

IV. THE FOOT OF A MOUNTAIN

V. A CABARET

VI. THE PRIVATE OFFICE

VII. OUTSIDE A TEMPLE

VIII. ANOTHER FISH FRY

THE
GREEN
PASTURES

PART ONE

PART ONE

SCENE I

A corner in a Negro church.

Ten children and an elderly preacher.

The costumes are those that might be seen in any lower Louisiana town at Sunday School time. As the curtain rises, MR. DESHEE, *the preacher, is reading from a Bible. The* CHILDREN *are listening with varied degrees of interest. Three or four are wide-eyed in their attention. Two or three are obviously puzzled, but interested, and the smallest ones are engaged in more physical concerns. One is playing with a little doll, and another runs his finger on all the angles of his chair.*

DESHEE: "An' Adam lived a hundred and thirty years, an' begat a son in his own likeness, after his image; an' called his name Seth. An' de days of Adam, after he had begotten Seth, were eight hundred years; an' he begat sons an' daughters; an' all de days dat Adam lived were nine hundred an' thirty years; an' he died. An' Seth lived a hundred an' five years an' begat Enos; an' Seth lived after he begat Enos eight hundred an' seven years and begat sons and daughters. An' all de days of Seth were nine hundred and twelve years; an'

3

he died." An' it go on like dat till we come to Enoch an' de book say: "An' Enoch lived sixty an' five years and begat Methuselah." Den it say: "An' all de days of Methuselah were nine hund'ed an' sixty an' nine years an' he died." An' dat was de oldest man dat ever was. Dat's why we call ol' Mr. Gurney's mammy ol' Mrs. Methuselah, caize she's so ol'. Den a little later it tell about another member of de fam'ly. His name was Noah. Maybe some of you know about him already. I'm gonter tell you all about him next Sunday. Anyway dat's de meat an' substance of de first five chapters of Genesis. Now, how you think you gonter like de Bible?

MYRTLE: I think it's jest wonderful, Mr. Deshee. I cain't understand any of it.

FIRST BOY: Why did dey live so long, Mr. Deshee?

DESHEE: Why? Caize dat was de way God felt.

SECOND BOY: Dat made Adam a way back.

DESHEE: Yes, he certainly 'way back by de time Noah come along. Want to ask me any mo' questions?

SECOND BOY: What de worl' look like when de Lawd begin, Mr. Deshee?

DESHEE: How yo' mean what it look like?

MYRTLE: Carlisle mean who was in N'Orleans den.

DESHEE: Dey wasn't nobody in N'Orleans on 'count dey wasn't any N'Orleans. Dat's de whole idea I tol' you at de end of de first Chapter. Yo' got to git yo' minds fixed. Dey wasn't any Rampart Street. Dey wasn't any Canal Street. Dey wasn't any Louisiana. Dey wasn't nothin' on de earth at all caize fo' de reason dey wasn't any earth.

MYRTLE: Yes, but what Carlisle wanter know is—

DESHEE: [*Interrupting and addressing little boy who has been playing with his chair and paying no attention.*] Now Randolph, if you don't listen, how yo' gonter grow up and be a good man? Yo' wanter grow up an' be a transgressor?

LITTLE BOY: [*Frightened.*] No.

DESHEE: You tell yo' mammy yo' sister got to come wid you next time. She

4

kin git de things done in time to bring you to de school. You content yo'self. [*The little boy straightens up in his chair*.] Now, what do Carlisle want to know?

CARLISLE: How he decide he want de worl' to be right yere and how he git de idea he wanted it?

MYRTLE: Caize de Book say, don't it, Mr. Deshee?

DESHEE: De Book say, but at de same time dat's a good question. I remember when I was a little boy de same thing recurred to me. An' ol' Mr. Dubois, he was a wonderful preacher at New Hope Chapel over in East Gretna, he said: "De answer is dat de Book ain't got time to go into all de details." And he was right. You know sometimes I think de Lawd expects us to figure out a few things for ourselves. We know that at one time dey wasn't anything except Heaven, we don't know jest where it was but we know it was dere. Maybe it was everywhere. Den one day de Lawd got the idea he'd like to make some places. He made de sun and de moon, de stars. An' he made de earth.

MYRTLE: Who was aroun' den, nothin' but angels?

DESHEE: I suppose so.

FIRST BOY: What was de angels doin' up dere?

DESHEE: I suppose dey jest flew aroun' and had a good time. Dey wasn't no sin, so dey musta had a good time.

FIRST BOY: Did dey have picnics?

DESHEE: Sho, dey had the nicest kind of picnics. Dey probably had fish frys, wid b'iled custard and ten cent seegars for de adults. God gives us humans lotsa ideas about havin' good times. Maybe dey were things he'd seen de angels do. Yes, sir, I bet dey had a fish fry every week.

MYRTLE: Did dey have Sunday School, too?

DESHEE: Yes, dey musta had Sunday School for de cherubs.

MYRTLE: What did God look like, Mr. Deshee?

DESHEE: Well, nobody knows exactly what God looked like. But when I was a little boy I used to imagine dat he looked like de Reverend Dubois. He was de finest looking ol' man I ever knew. Yes, I used to bet de Lawd looked exactly

5

like Mr. Dubois in de days when he walked de earth in de shape of a natchel man.

MYRTLE: When was dat, Mr. Deshee?

DESHEE: Why, when he was gettin' things started down heah. When He talked to Adam and Eve and Noah and Moses and all dem. He made mighty men in dem days. But aldo they was awful mighty dey always knew dat He was beyond dem all. Pretty near one o'clock, time fo' you chillun to go home to dinner, but before I let you go I wan' you to go over wid me de main facts of de first lesson. What's de name of de book?

CHILDREN: Genesis.

DESHEE: Dat's right. And what's de other name?

CHILDREN: First Book of Moses.

DESHEE: Dat's right. And dis yere's Chapter One. [*The lights begin to dim.*] "In de beginnin' God created de heaven an' de earth. An' de earth was widout form an' void. An' de darkness was upon de face of de deep."

SCENE II

In the darkness many voices are heard singing
"Oh, Rise an' Shine, Give God the Glory."

Oh, rise an' shine
An' give God de glory, glory,
 Rise an' shine,
Give God de glory, glory,
 Rise an' shine,
An' give God de glory, glory,
For de year of Jubilee.

Oh, come on, Mo'ner,
An' get you ready, ready.
 Come on, Mo'ner,
An' get you ready, ready.
 Come on, Mo'ner,
An' get you ready, ready,
For de year of Jubilee.

Oh, come on, chillun,
An' don' be weary, weary.
 Come on, chillun,
An' don' be weary, weary.
 Come on, chillun,
An' don' be weary, weary,
For de year of Jubilee.

They sing it gayly and rapidly. The lights go up as the second verse ends. The chorus is being sung diminuendo by a mixed company of angels. That is they are angels in that they

7

wear brightly colored robes and have wings protruding from their backs. Otherwise they look and act like a company of happy negroes at a fish fry. The scene itself is a pre-Creation Heaven with compromises. In the distance is an unbroken stretch of blue sky. Companionable varicolored clouds billow down to the floor of the stage and roll overhead to the branches of a live oak tree which is up left. The tree is leafy and dripping with Spanish moss, and with the clouds makes a frame for the scene. In the cool shade of the tree are the usual appurtenances of a fish fry; a large kettle of hot fat set on two small parallel logs, with a fire going underneath, and a large rustic table formed by driving four stakes into the ground and placing planks on top of the small connecting boards. On the table are piles of biscuits and corn bread and the cooked fish in dish pans. There are one or two fairly large cedar or crock "churns" containing boiled custard, which looks like milk. There is a gourd dipper beside the churns and several glasses and cups of various sizes and shapes from which the custard is drunk.

The principal singers are marching two by two in a small area at the R of the stage. Two MAMMY ANGELS *are attending to the frying beside the kettle. Behind the table a* MAN ANGEL *is skinning fish and passing them to the cooks. Another is ladling out the custard. A* MAMMY ANGEL *is putting fish on bread for a brood of cherubs, and during the first scene they seat themselves on a grassy bank upstage. Another* MAMMY ANGEL *is clapping her hands disapprovingly and beckoning a laughing* BOY CHERUB *down from a cloud a little out of her reach. Another* MAMMY ANGEL *is solicitously slapping the back of a girl cherub who has a large fish sandwich in her hand and a bone in her throat. There is much movement about the table, and during the first few minutes several individuals go up to the table to help themselves to the food and drink. Many of the women angels wear hats and a few of the men are smoking cigars. A large boxful is on the table. There is much laughter and chatter as the music softens, but continues, during the early part of the action. The following short scenes are played almost simultaneously.*

FIRST COOK: [*At kettle. Calling off.*] Hurry up, Cajey. Dis yere fat's cryin' fo' mo' feesh.

A VOICE: [*Off stage.*] We comin', fas' we kin. Dey got to be ketched, ain't

8

dey? We cain't say. "C'm'on little fish. C'm'on an' git fried," kin we?

SECOND COOK: [*At table.*] De trouble is de mens is all worm fishin'.

FIRST MAN ANGEL: [*At table.*] Whut dif'runce do it make? Yo' all de time got to make out like somebody's doin' somethin' de wrong way.

SECOND COOK: [*Near table.*] I s'pose you got de per'fec' way fo' makin' bait.

FIRST MAN ANGEL: I ain't sayin' dat. I is sayin' whut's wrong wid worm fishin'.

SECOND COOK: Whut's wrong wid worm fishin'? Ever'thing, dat's all. Dey's only one good way fo' catfishin', an' dat's minny fishin'. Anybody know dat.

FIRST MAN ANGEL: Well, it jest so happen dat minny fishin' is de dog-gondest fool way of fishin' dey is. You kin try minny fishin' to de cows come home an' all you catch'll be de backache. De trouble wid you, sister, is you jest got minny fishin' on de brain.

SECOND COOK: Go right on, loud mouf. You tell me de news. My, my! You jest de wisest person in de worl'. First you, den de Lawd God.

FIRST MAN ANGEL: [*To the custard ladler.*] You cain't tell dem nothin'. [*Walks away to the custard churn.*] Does you try to 'splain some simple fac' dey git man-deaf.

FIRST MAMMY ANGEL: [*To* CHERUB *on the cloud.*] Now, you heerd me. [*The* CHERUB *assumes several mocking poses, as she speaks.*] You fly down yere. You wanter be put down in de sin book? [*She goes to the table, gets a drink for herself and points out the cherub to one of the men behind the table.*] Dat baby must got imp blood in him he so vexin'. [*She returns to her position under the cloud.*] You want me to fly up dere an' slap you down? Now, I tol' you. [*The* CHERUB *starts to come down.*]

STOUT ANGEL: [*To the* CHERUB *with a bone in her throat.*] I tol' you you was too little fo' cat fish. What you wanter git a bone in yo' froat fo'? [*She slaps the* CHERUB'S *back.*]

11

SLENDER ANGEL: [*Leisurely eating a sandwich as she watches the backslapping.*] What de trouble wid Leonetta?

STOUT ANGEL: She got a catfish bone down her froat. [*To the* CHERUB.] Doggone, I tol' you to eat grinnel instead.

SLENDER ANGEL: Ef'n she do git all dat et, she gonter have de bellyache.

STOUT ANGEL: Ain't I tol' her dat? [*To* CHERUB.] Come on now; let go dat bone. [*She slaps* CHERUB'S *back again. The bone is dislodged and the* CHERUB *grins her relief.*] Dat's good.

SLENDER ANGEL: [*Comfortingly.*] Now she all right.

STOUT ANGEL: Go on an' play wid yo' cousins. [*The* CHERUB *joins the Cherubs sitting on the embankment. The concurrency of scenes ends here.*] I ain't see you lately, Lily. How you been?

SLENDER ANGEL: Me, I'm fine. I been visitin' my mammy. She waitin' on de welcome table over by de throne of grace.

STOUT ANGEL: She always was pretty holy.

SLENDER ANGEL: Yes, ma'am. She like it dere. I guess de Lawd's took quite a fancy to her.

STOUT ANGEL: Well, dat's natural. I declare yo' mammy one of de finest lady angels I know.

SLENDER ANGEL: She claim you de best one she know.

STOUT ANGEL: Well, when you come right down to it, I suppose we is all pretty near perfec'.

SLENDER ANGEL: Yes, ma'am. Why is dat, Mis' Jenny?

STOUT ANGEL: I s'pose it's caize de Lawd he don' 'low us 'sociatin' wid de devil any mo' so dat dey cain' be no mo' sinnin'.

SLENDER ANGEL: Po' ol' Satan. Whutevah become of him?

STOUT ANGEL: De Lawd put him some place I s'pose.

SLENDER ANGEL: But dey ain't any place but Heaven, is dey?

STOUT ANGEL: De Lawd could make a place, couldn't he?

SLENDER ANGEL: Dat's de truth. Dey's one thing confuses me though.

12

STOUT ANGEL: What's dat?

SLENDER ANGEL: I do a great deal of travelin' an' I ain't never come across any place but Heaven anywhere. So if de Lawd kick Satan out of Heaven jest whereat did he go? Dat's my question.

STOUT ANGEL: You bettah let de Lawd keep his own secrets, Lily. De way things is goin' now dey ain't been no sinnin' since dey give dat scamp a kick in de pants. Nowadays Heaven's free of sin an' if a lady wants a little constitutional she kin fly 'til she wing-weary widout gittin' insulted.

SLENDER ANGEL: I was jest a baby when Satan lef'. I don't even 'member what he look like.

STOUT ANGEL: He was jest right fo' a devil. [*An* ARCHANGEL *enters. He is older than the others and wears a white beard. His clothing is much darker than that of the others and his wings a trifle more imposing.*] Good mo'nin', Archangel. [*Others say good morning.*]

ARCHANGEL: Good mo'nin', folks. I wonder kin I interrup' de fish fry an' give out de Sunday school cyards? [*Cries of "Suttingly!" "Mah goodness, yes"— etc. The marching* CHOIR *stops.*] You kin keep singin' if you want to. Why don' you sing "When de Saints Come Marchin' In?" Seem to me I ain' heard dat lately. [*The* CHOIR *begins "When the Saints Come Marching In,"*

When de Saints come marchin' in,
When de Saints come marchin' in
Lord, I want to be in dat number,
When de Saints come marchin' in.

I have a lovin' brother,
He has gone on befo'
An' I promised I would meet Him
When dey crown Him Lord of all.

13

When dey crown Him Lord of all,
When dey crown Him Lord of all,
Lord, I want to be in dat number
When dey crown Him Lord of all.

rather softly, but does not resume marching. The ARCHANGEL *looks off left.*] All right, bring 'em yere. [*A prim looking* WOMAN TEACHER-ANGEL *enters, shepherding ten* BOY *and* GIRL CHERUBS. *The* TEACHER *carries ten beribboned diplomas, which she gives to the* ARCHANGEL. *The cherubs are dressed in stiffly starched white suits and dresses, the little girls having enormous ribbons at the backs of their dresses and smaller ones in their hair and on the tips of their wings. They line up in front of the archangel and receive the attention of the rest of the company. The* CHOIR *sings through the ceremony.*] Now den cherubs, why is you yere?

CHILDREN: Because we so good.

ARCHANGEL: Dat's right. Now who de big boss?

CHILDREN: Our dear Lawd.

ARCHANGEL: Dat's right. When you all grow up what you gonter be?

CHILDREN: Holy angels at de throne of grace.

ARCHANGEL: Dat's right. Now, you passed yo' 'xaminations and it gives me great pleasure to hand out de cyards for de whole class. Gineeva Chaproe. [*The* FIRST GIRL CHERUB *goes to him and gets her diploma. The* CHOIR *sings loudly and resumes marching, as the* ARCHANGEL *calls out another name—and presents diplomas.*] Corey Moulter. [SECOND GIRL CHERUB *gets her diploma.*] Nootzie Winebush. [THIRD GIRL CHERUB.] Harriet Prancy. [FOURTH GIRL CHERUB] I guess you is Brozain Stew't. [*He gives the* FIFTH GIRL CHERUB *the paper. Each of the presentations has been accompanied by hand-clapping from the bystanders.*] Now you boys know yo' own names. Suppose you come yere and help me git dese 'sorted right?

[BOY CHERUBS *gather about him and receive their diplomas. The little* GIRLS *have scattered about the stage, joining groups of the adult angels. The angel* GABRIEL *enters.*

14

He is bigger and more elaborately winged than even the Archangel, but he is also much younger and beardless. His costume is less conventional than that of the other men, resembling more the Gabriel of the Doré drawings. His appearance causes a flutter among the others. They stop their chattering with the children. The CHOIR *stops as three or four audible whispers of "Gabriel!" are heard. In a moment the heavenly company is all attention.*]

GABRIEL: [*Lifting his hand.*] Gangway! Gangway for de Lawd God Jehovah!

[*There is a reverent hush and* GOD *enters. He is the tallest and biggest of them all. He wears a white shirt with a white bow tie, a long Prince Albert coat of black alpaca, black trousers and congress gaiters. He looks at the assemblage. There is a pause. He speaks in a rich, bass voice.*]

GOD: Is you been baptized?

OTHERS: [*Chanting.*] Certainly, Lawd.

GOD: Is you been baptized?

OTHERS: Certainly, Lawd.

GOD: [*With the beginning of musical notation.*] Is you been baptized?

OTHERS: [*Now half-singing.*] Certainly, Lawd. Certainly, certainly, certainly, Lawd.

[*They sing the last two verses with equivalent part division.*]

Is you been redeemed?
  Cert'n'y, Lawd.
Is you been redeemed?
  Cert'n'y, Lawd.
Is you been redeemed?
  Cert'n'y, Lawd. Cert'n'y,
    cert'n'y, cert'n'y, Lawd.

Do you bow mighty low?
  Cert'n'y, Lawd.
Do you bow mighty low?
  Cert'n'y, Lawd.
Do you bow mighty low?
  Cert'n'y, Lawd. Cert'n'y,
    cert'n'y, cert'n'y, Lawd.

[*As the last response ends all heads are bowed. God looks at them for a moment; then lifts His hand.*]

GOD: Let de fish fry proceed.

[EVERYONE *rises. The* ANGELS *relax and resume their inaudible conversations. The activity behind the table and about the cauldron is resumed. Some of the choir members cross to the table and get sandwiches and cups of the boiled custard. Three or four of the children in the Sunday School class and the little girl who had the bone in her throat affectionately group themselves about God as he speaks with the Archangel. He pats their heads, they hang to his coat-tails, etc.*]

ARCHANGEL: Good mo'nin', Lawd.

GOD: Good mo'nin', Deacon. You lookin' pretty spry.

ARCHANGEL: I cain' complain. We just been givin' our cyards to de chillun.

GOD: Dat's good. [*A small cherub, his feet braced against one of God's shoes is using God's coat-tail as a trapeze. One of the* COOKS *offers a fish sandwich which* GOD *politely declines.*]

FIRST MAMMY ANGEL: Now, you leave go de Lawd's coat, Herman. You heah me?

GOD: Dat's all right, sister. He jest playin'.

FIRST MAMMY ANGEL: He playin' too rough. [GOD *picks up the cherub and spanks him good-naturedly. The* CHERUB *squeals with delight and runs to his mother.* GABRIEL *advances to* GOD *with a glass of the custard.*]

GABRIEL: Little b'iled custud, Lawd?

GOD: Thank you very kindly. Dis looks nice.

CUSTARD MAKER: [*Offering a box.*] Ten cent seegar, Lawd?

GOD: [*Taking it.*] Thank you, thank you. How de fish fry goin'? [*Ad lib. cries of* "O. K. Lawd," "Fine an' dandy, Lawd," "De best one yit, Lawd," *etc. To the choir.*] How you shouters gittin' on?

CHOIR LEADER: We been marchin' and singin' de whole mo'nin'.

GOD: I heerd you. You gittin' better all de time. You gittin' as good as de one at de throne. Why don' you give us one dem ol' time jump-ups?

CHOIR LEADER: Anythin' you say, Lawd. [*To the others.*] "So High!"

16

[*The* CHOIR *begins to sing* "*My God Is So High You Can't Get Over Him.*"

> My God is so High
> You can't git over Him,
> He's so low, you can't git under Him,
> He's so wide, you can't git around Him
> You mus' come in, right through de Lam'.
>
> My God is so High
> You can't git over Him,
> He's so low, you can't git under Him,
> He's so wide, you can't git around Him
> You mus' come in, right through de Lam'.
>
> One day as I was a-walkin'
> Along de Heb'n'ly road,
> My Saviour spoke unto me
> An' He filled my heart wid love.
>
> My God is so High
> You can't git over Him,
> He's so low, you can't git under Him,
> He's so wide, you can't git around Him
> You mus' come in, right through de Lam'.

They sing softly, but do not march. An ANGEL *offers his cigar to* GOD *from which He can light His own.*]

GOD: No thanks. I'm gonter save dis a bit. [*He puts the cigar in his pocket and listens to the singers a moment. Then he sips his custard. After the second sip, a look of displeasure comes on his face.*]

GABRIEL: What's de matter, Lawd?

GOD: [*Sipping again.*] I ain't jest sure, yit. Dey's something 'bout dis custahd. [*Takes another sip.*]

CUSTARD MAKER: Ain't it all right, Lawd?

GOD: It don't seem seasoned jest right. You make it?

CUSTARD MAKER: Yes, Lawd, I put everythin' in it like I allus do. It's supposed to be perfec'.

GOD: Yeah. I kin taste de eggs and de cream and de sugar. [*Suddenly.*] I know what it is. It needs jest a little bit mo' firmament.

CUSTARD MAKER: Dey's firmament in it, Lawd.

GOD: Maybe, but it ain' enough.

CUSTARD MAKER: It's all we had, Lawd. Dey ain't a drap in de jug.

GOD: Dat's all right. I'll jest r'ar back an' pass a miracle. [CHOIR *stops singing.*] Let it be some firmament! An' when I say let it be some firmament, I don't want jest a little bitty dab o' firmament caize I'm sick an' tired of runnin' out of it when we need it. Let it be a whole mess of firmament! [*The stage has become misty until* GOD *and the heavenly company are obscured. As he finishes the speech there is a burst of thunder. As the stage grows darker.*] Dat's de way I like it. [*Murmurs from the others; "Dat's a lot of firmament." "My, dat is firmament!" "Look to me like he's created rain," etc.*]

FIRST MAMMY ANGEL: [*When the stage is dark.*] Now, look Lawd, dat's too much firmament. De Cherubs is gettin' all wet.

SECOND MAMMY ANGEL: Look at my Carlotta, Lawd. She's soaked to de skin. Dat's *plenty* too much firmament.

GOD: Well, 'co'se we don't want de chillun to ketch cold. Can't you dreen it off?

GABRIEL: Dey's no place to dreen it, Lawd.

FIRST MAMMY ANGEL: Why don't we jest take de babies home, Lawd?

GOD: No, I don' wanta bust up de fish fry. You angels keep quiet an' I'll pass another miracle. Dat's always de trouble wid miracles. When you pass one

18

you always gotta r'ar back an' pass another. [*There is a hush.*] Let dere be a place to dreen off dis firmament. Let dere be mountains and valleys an' let dere be oceans an' lakes. An' let dere be rivers and bayous to dreen it off in, too. As a matter of fac' let dere be de earth. An' when dat's done let dere be de sun, an' let it come out and dry my Cherubs' wings.

[*The lights go up until the stage is bathed in sunlight. On the embankment upstage there is now a waist-high wrought iron railing such as one sees on the galleries of houses in the French quarter of New Orleans. The* CHERUBS *are being examined by their parents and there is an ad lib. murmur of, "You all right, honey?" "You feel better now, Albert?" "Now you all dry, Vangy?" until the* ARCHANGEL, *who has been gazing in awe at the railing, drowns them out.*]

ARCHANGEL: Look yere! [*There is a rush to the embankment accompanied by exclamations, "My goodness!" "What's dis?" "I declah!" etc.* GABRIEL *towers above the group on the middle of the embankment.* GOD *is wrapped in thought, facing the audience. The* CHOIR *sings "Hallelujah."*]

> Hallelujah, an'-a Hallelujah!
> Hallelujah, Lord,
> I been down into de sea.
>
> Hallelujah, an'-a Hallelujah!
> Hallelujah, Lord,
> I been down into de sea.

The babbling at the balustrade dies away as the people lean over the railing. GABRIEL *turns and faces* GOD *indicating the earth below the railing with his left hand.*]

GABRIEL: Do you see it, Lawd?

GOD: [*Quietly, without turning his head upstage.*] Yes, Gabriel.

GABRIEL: Looks mighty nice, Lawd.

GOD: Yes. [GABRIEL *turns and looks over the railing.*]

GABRIEL: [*Gazing down.*] Yes, suh. Dat'd make mighty nice farming country. Jest look at dat South forty over dere. You ain't going to let dat go to waste is you, Lawd? Dat would be a pity an' a shame.

GOD: [*Not turning.*] It's a good earth. [GOD *turns, room is made for him beside* GABRIEL *on the embankment.*] Yes. I ought to have somebody to enjoy it. [*He turns, facing the audience. The others, save for the choir who are lined up in two rows of six on an angle up right, continue to look over the embankment.*] Gabriel! [GOD *steps down from the embankment two paces.*]

GABRIEL: [*Joining him.*] Yes, Lawd.

GOD: Gabriel, I'm goin' down dere.

GABRIEL: Yes, Lawd.

GOD: I want you to be my working boss yere while I'm gone.

GABRIEL: Yes, Lawd.

GOD: You know dat matter of dem two stars?

GABRIEL: Yes, Lawd.

GOD: Git dat fixed up! You know dat sparrow dat fell a little while ago? 'Tend to dat, too.

GABRIEL: Yes, Lawd.

GOD: I guess dat's about all. I'll be back Saddy. [*To the* CHOIR.] Quiet, angels. [*The* CHOIR *stops singing. Those on the embankment circle down stage.* GOD *goes to embankment. Turns and faces the company.*] I'm gonter pass one more miracle. You all gonter help me an' not make a soun' caize it's one of de most impo'tant miracles of all. [*Nobody moves.* GOD *turns, facing the sky and raises his arms above his head.*] Let there be man.

[*There is growing roll of thunder as stage grows dark. The* CHOIR *bursts into "In Bright Mansions Above,"*

> In bright mansions above,
>   In bright mansions above,
> Lord, I want to live up yonder
>   In bright mansions above.

My mother's gone to glory,
　　I want to go there, too,
Lord, I want to live up yonder
　　In bright mansions above.

In bright mansions above,
　　In bright mansions above,
Lord, I want to live up yonder
　　In bright mansions above.

and continues until the lights go up on the next scene.]

SCENE III

*Enclosing the stage is a heterogeneous cluster of cottonwood, camphor, live oak and syca-
more trees, youpon and turkey berry bushes, with their purple and red berries, sprays of
fern-like indigo fiera and splashes of various Louisiana flowers. In the middle of the stage,
disclosed when the mistiness at rise grows into warm sunlight, stands* ADAM. *He is a
puzzled man of 30, of medium height, dressed in the clothing of the average field hand.
He is bare-headed. In the distance can be heard the choir continuing. "Bright Mansions
Above." A bird begins to sing.* ADAM *smiles and turns to look at the source of this novel
sound. He senses his strength and raises his forearms, his fists clenched. With his left hand
he carefully touches the muscles of his upper right arm. He smiles again, realizing his
power. He looks at his feet which are stretched wide apart. He stamps once or twice and
now almost laughs in his enjoyment. Other birds begin trilling and* ADAM *glances up
joyfully toward the foliage.* GOD *enters.*

GOD: Good mo'nin', Son.

ADAM: [*With a little awe.*] Good mo'nin', Lawd.

GOD: What's yo' name, Son?

ADAM: Adam.

GOD: Adam which?

ADAM: [*Frankly, after a moment's puzzled groping.*] Jest Adam, Lawd.

GOD: Well, Adam, how dey treatin' you? How things goin'?

ADAM: Well, Lawd, you know it's kind of a new line of wukk.

GOD: You'll soon get de hang of it. You know yo' kind of a new style with me.

ADAM: Oh, I guess I'm gonter make out all right soon as I learn de ropes.

GOD: Yes, I guess you will. Yo' a nice job.

ADAM: Yes, Lawd.

GOD: Dey's jest one little thing de matter with you. Did you notice it?

ADAM: Well, now you mentioned it, Lawd, I kind of thought dey was somethin' wrong.

GOD: Yes suh, you ain't quite right. Adam, you need a family. De reason for dat is in yo' heart you is a family man. [*Flicking the ash off his cigar.*] I'd say dat was de main trouble at de moment.

ADAM: [*Smiling.*] Yes sir. [*His smile fades and he is puzzled again.*] At de same time—dey's one thing puzzlin' me, Lawd. Could I ask you a question?

GOD: Why, certainly, Adam.

ADAM: Lawd, jest what *is* a family?

GOD: I'm gonter show you. [*Indicates a spot.*] Jest lie down dere, Adam. Make out like you was goin' to slumber.

ADAM: [*Gently.*] Yes, Lawd.

[*He lies down.* GOD *stands beside him and as he raises his arms above his head the lights go down. In the darkness* GOD *speaks.*]

GOD: Eve. [*Lights go up.* EVE *is standing beside* ADAM. *She is about twenty-six, and quite pretty. She is dressed like a country girl. Her gingham dress is quite new and clean.* GOD *is now at the other side of the stage, looking at them critically.* EVE *looks at* ADAM *in timid wonder and slowly turns her head until she meets the glance of* GOD. ADAM *stands beside* EVE. *They gaze at each other for a moment.* GOD *smiles.*] Now you all right, Eve. [ADAM *and* EVE *face him.*] Now I'll tell you what I'm gonter do. I'm gonter put you in charge here. I'm gonter give you de run of dis whole garden. Eve, you take care of dis man an' Adam you take care of dis

24

woman. You belong to each other. I don' want you to try to do too much caize yo' both kind of experiment wid me an' I ain't sho' whether you could make it. You two jest enjoy yo'self. Drink de water from de little brooks an' de wine from de grapes an' de berries, an'eat de food dat's hangin' for you in de trees. [*He pauses, startled by a painful thought.*] Dat is, in all but one tree. [*He pauses. Then, not looking at them.*] You know what I mean, my children?

ADAM AND EVE: Yes, Lawd. [*They slowly turn their heads left, toward the branches of an offstage tree. Then they look back at* GOD.]

ADAM: Thank you, Lawd.

EVE: Thank you, Lawd.

GOD: I gotter be gittin' along now. I got a hund'ed thousan' things to do 'fo' you take yo' nex' breath. Enjoy yo'selves——

[GOD *exits.*]

[ADAM *and* EVE *stand looking after Him for a moment, then each looks down and watches their hands meet and clasp.*]

[*After a moment they lift their heads slowly until they are again gazing at the tree.*]

EVE: Adam.

ADAM: [*Looking at the tree, almost in terror.*] What?

EVE: [*Softly as she too continues to look at the tree.*] Adam.

[*The* CHOIR *begins singing "Turn You Roun'"*

Don't you let nobody turn you roun'
Turn you roun', turn you roun',
Don't you let nobody turn you roun'
Keep away from de Ed'n tree.

Ol' Sat'n's a liar an' a cunjer too,
Keep away from de Ed'n tree;
If you don' min' out he'll cunjer you,
Keep away from de Ed'n tree.

27

Don't you let nobody turn you roun'
Turn you roun', turn you roun',
Don't you let nobody turn you roun'
Keep away from de Ed'n tree.

Don't you let nobody turn you roun'
Turn you roun', turn you roun',
Don't you let nobody turn you roun'
Keep away from de Ed'n tree.

and as the lights go down the CHOIR *continues until there is blackness. The* CHOIR *suddenly stops. The following scene is played in the darkness.*]

MR. DESHEE'S VOICE: Now, I s'pose you chillun know what happened after God made Adam 'n' Eve. Do you?

FIRST GIRL'S VOICE: I know, Mr. Deshee.

MR. DESHEE'S VOICE: Jest a minute, Randolph. Didn't I tell you you gotta tell yo' mammy let yo' sister bring you? Carlisle, take way dat truck he's eatin'. You sit by him, see kin you keep him quiet. Now, den, Myrtle, what happened?

FIRST GIRL'S VOICE: Why, den dey ate de fo'bidden fruit and den dey got driv' out de garden.

MR. DESHEE'S VOICE: An' den what happened?

FIRST GIRL'S VOICE: Den dey felt ver bad.

MR. DESHEE'S VOICE: I don' mean how dey feel, I mean how dey do. Do dey have any children or anything like dat?

FIRST GIRL'S VOICE: Oh, yes, suh, dey have Cain 'n' Abel.

MR. DESHEE'S VOICE: Dat's right, dey have Cain an' Abel.

BOY'S VOICE: Dat was a long time after dey got married, wasn't it, Mr. Deshee? My mammy say it was a hund'ed years.

MR. DESHEE'S VOICE: Well, nobody kin be so sure. As I tol' you befo'

28

dey was jest beginnin' to be able to tell de time an' nobody was any too sure 'bout anythin' even den. So de bes' thing to do is jest realize dat de thing happened an' don't bother 'bout how many years it was. Jest remember what I told you about it gittin' dark when you go to sleep an' it bein' light when you wake up. Dat's de way time went by in dem days. One thing we do know an' dat was dis boy Cain was a mean rascal. [*The lights go up on the next scene.*]

SCENE IV

A roadside.

CAIN, *a husky young Negro, stands over the body of the dead* ABEL. *Both are dressed as laborers.* CAIN *is looking at the body in awe, a rock in his right hand.* GOD *enters.*

GOD: Cain, look what you done to Abel.

CAIN: Lawd, I was min'in' my own business and he come monkeyin' aroun' wit' me. I was wukkin' in de fiel' an' he was sittin' in de shade of de tree. He say "Me, I'd be skeered to git out in dis hot sun. I be 'fraid my brains gits cooked. Co'se you ain't got no brains so you ain' in no danger." An' so I up and flang de rock. If it miss 'im all right, an' if it hit 'im, all right. Dat's de way I feel.

GOD: All right, but I'm yere to tell you dat's called a crime. When de new Judge is done talkin' to you you'll be draggin' a ball and chain de rest of yo' life.

CAIN: Well, what'd he want to come monkeyin' aroun' me fo' den? I was jest plowin', min'in' my own business, and not payin' him no min', and yere he come makin' me de fool. I'd bust anybody what make me de fool.

GOD: Well, I ain't sayin' you right an' I ain't sayin' you wrong. But I do say was I you I'd jest git myself down de road 'til I was clean out of de county.

31

An' you better take an' git married an' settle down an' raise some chillun. Dey ain't nothin' to make a man fo'git his troubles like raisin' a family. Now, you better git.

CAIN: Yessuh.

[CAIN *walks off.*]

[GOD *watches him from the forestage and as the lights begin to dim looks off. The* CHOIR *begins "Run, Sinner, Run."*]

> Run sinner run, hunt you a hidin' place,
> Run sinner run, hunt you a hidin' place,
> Run sinner run, hunt you a hidin' place,
> In-a dat mornin', oh, my Lord,
> In-a dat mornin', oh, my Lord,
> In-a dat mornin', when de Lord say "Hurry."
>
> Oh, Gab'l strike dat 'vidin' line,
> Oh, Gab'l strike dat 'vidin' line,
> Oh, Gab'l strike dat 'vidin' line,
> In-a dat mornin', oh, my Lord,
> In-a dat mornin', oh, my Lord,
> In-a dat mornin', when de Lord say "Hurry."
>
> Run sinner run, hunt you a hidin' place,
> Run sinner run, hunt you a hidin' place,
> Run sinner run, hunt you a hidin' place,
> In-a dat mornin', oh, my Lord,
> In-a dat mornin', oh, my Lord,
> In-a dat mornin' when de Lord say "Hurry."

GOD: Adam an' Eve you better try again. You better have Seth an' a lot mo' chillun.

[*There is darkness. The* CHOIR *continues until the lights go up on the next scene.*]

32

SCENE V

CAIN *is discovered walking on an unseen treadmill. A middle distance of trees, hillsides and shrubbery passes him on an upper treadmill. Behind is the blue sky. He stops under the branches of a tree to look at a sign on a fence railing. Only half the tree is visible on the stage. The sign reads,* "NOD PARISH. COUNTY LINE."

CAIN: [*Sitting down with a sigh of relief under the tree.*] At las'! Phew![*Wipes his forehead with a handkerchief.*] Feels like I been walkin' fo'ty years. [*He looks back.*] Well, dey cain' git me now. Now I kin raise a fam'ly. [*An idea occurs to him, and suddenly he begins looking right and left.*] Well, I'll be hit by a mule! Knock me down for a trustin' baby! Where I gonter git dat fam'ly? Dat preacher fooled me. [*He is quite dejected.*] Doggone!

CAIN'S GIRL: [*Off stage.*] Hello, Country Boy!

[CAIN *glances up to the offstage branches of the tree.*]

CAIN: Hey-ho, Good lookin'! Which way is it to de town?

CAIN'S GIRL: [*Off stage.*] What you tryin' to do? You tryin' to mash me? I be doggone if it ain't gittin' so a gal cain't hardly leave de house 'out some of dese fast men ain' passin' remarks at her.

CAIN: I ain' passin' remarks.

35

CAIN'S GIRL: [*Off stage.*] If I thought you was tryin' to mash me, I'd call de police an' git you tooken to de first precinct.

CAIN: Look yere, gal, I ast you a question, an' if you don' answer me I'm gonter bend you 'cross my pants an' burn you up.

CAIN'S GIRL: [*Off stage.*] I'm comin' down.

[CAIN *takes his eyes from the tree.*]

CAIN: Yes, an' you better hurry.

[CAIN'S GIRL *enters. She is as large as* CAIN, *wickedly pretty, and somewhat flashily dressed. She smiles at* CAIN.]

CAIN'S GIRL: I bet you kin handle a gal mean wid dem big stout arms of your'n. I sho' would hate to git you mad at me, Country Boy.

CAIN: [*Smiling.*] Come yere. [*She goes a little closer to him.*] Don't be 'fraid, I ain' so mean.

CAIN'S GIRL: You got two bad lookin' eyes. I bet yo' hot coffee 'mong de women folks.

CAIN: I ain' never find out. What was you doin' in dat tree?

CAIN'S GIRL: Jes coolin' myself in de element.

CAIN: Is you a Nod Parish gal?

CAIN'S GIRL: Bo'n an' bred.

CAIN: You know yo' kinda pretty.

CAIN'S GIRL: Who tol' you dat?

CAIN: Dese yere two bad eyes of mine.

CAIN'S GIRL: I bet you say dat to everybody all de way down de road.

CAIN: Comin' down dat road I didn't talk to nobody.

CAIN'S GIRL: Where you boun' for, Beautiful?

CAIN: I'm jest seein' de country. I thought I might settle down yere fo' a spell. You live wit' yo' people?

CAIN'S GIRL: Co'se I does.

CAIN: 'Spose dey'd like to take in a boarder?

CAIN'S GIRL: Be nice if dey would, wouldn't it?

36

CAIN: I think so. You got a beau?

CAIN'S GIRL: [*With a negative shake of her head.*] Huh-uh!

CAIN: [*Smiling.*] You has *now*.

CAIN'S GIRL: I guess—I guess if you wanted to kiss me an' I tried to stop you, you could pretty nearly crush me wit' dem stout arms.

CAIN: You wouldn't try too much, would you?

CAIN'S GIRL: Maybe for a little while.

CAIN: An' den what?

CAIN'S GIRL: Why don' we wait an' see?

CAIN: When would dat be?

CAIN'S GIRL: Tonight. After supper. Think you kin walk a little further now, City Boy?

CAIN: Yeh, I ain't so weary now.

[*She takes his hand.*]

CAIN'S GIRL: What yo' name? [*Takes his arm.*]

CAIN: Cain.

CAIN'S GIRL: Then I'm Cain's Gal. Come on, honey, an' meet de folks.

[*They exit.*]

[*The* choir *is heard singing "You Better Min'," as* GOD *enters.*]

> Oh, you better min',
> Oh, you better min',
> You got to give an account at de Jedgment,
> You better min'.

> Oh, you better min',
> Oh, you better min',
> You got to give an account at de Jedgment,
> You better min'.

You better min' how you talk,
You better min' what you talkin' about;
You got to give an account at de Jedgment,
    You better min'.

You better min' how you sin,
You better min' what you singin' about,
You got to give an account at de Jedgment,
    You better min'.

Oh, you better min',
Oh, you better min',
You got to give an account at de Jedgment,
You better min'.

Oh, you better min',
Oh, you better min',
You got to give an account at de Jedgment,
You better min'.

[GOD *watches the vanished* CAIN *and his girl.*]
GOD: [*After shaking his head.*] Bad business. I don' like de way things is goin'
atall. [*The stage is darkened. The* CHOIR *continues singing until the lights go up on
the next scene.*]

SCENE VI

GOD'S *private office in Heaven. It is a small room, framed by tableau curtains. A large window up center looks out on the sky. There is a battered roll-top desk. On the wall next to the window is a framed religious oleograph with a calendar attached to it underneath. A door is at the left. A hat rack is on the wall above the door. There are two or three cheap pine chairs beside the window, and beyond the door. In front of the desk is an old swivel armchair which creaks every time* GOD *leans back in it. The desk is open and various papers are stuck in the pigeonholes. Writing implements, etc. are on the desk. On a shelf above the desk is a row of law books. A cuspidor is near the desk, and a waste basket by it. The general atmosphere is that of the office of a Negro lawyer in a Louisiana town. As the lights go up* GOD *takes a fresh cigar from a box on the desk and begins puffing it without bothering to light it. There is no comment on this minor miracle from* GABRIEL *who is sitting in one of the chairs with a pencil and several papers in his hand. The singing becomes pianissimo.*

GABRIEL: [*Looking at the papers.*] Well, I guess dat's about all de impo'tant business this mornin', Lawd.

39

GOD: How 'bout dat Cherub over to Archangel Montgomery's house?

GABRIEL: Where do dey live, Lawd?

[*The singing stops.*]

GOD: Dat little two story gold house, over by de pearly gates.

GABRIEL: Oh, *dat* Montgomery. I thought you was referrin' to de ol' gentleman. Oh, yeh. [*He sorts through the papers and finds one he is looking for.*] Yere it 'tis. [*Reads.*] "Cherub Christina Montgomery; wings is moltin' out of season an' nobody knows what to do."

GOD: Well, now, take keer of dat. You gotter be more careful, Gabe.

GABRIEL: Yes, Lawd.

[*Folds the papers and puts them in a pocket.* GOD *turns to his desk, takes another puff or two of the cigar, and with a pencil, begins checking off items on a sheet of paper before him. His back is turned toward* GABRIEL. GABRIEL *takes his trumpet from the hat rack and burnishes it with his robe. He then wets his lips and puts the mouthpiece to his mouth.*]

GOD: [*Without turning around.*] Now, watch yo'self, Gabriel.

GABRIEL: I wasn't goin' to blow, Lawd. I jest do dat every now an' den so I can keep de feel of it.

[*He leans trumpet against the wall.* GOD *picks up the papers and swings his chair around toward* GABRIEL.]

GOD: What's dis yere about de moon?

GABRIEL: [*Suddenly remembering.*] Oh! De moon people say it's beginnin' to melt a little, on 'count caize de sun's so hot.

GOD: It's goin' 'roun' 'cordin' to schedule, ain't it?

GABRIEL: Yes, Lawd.

GOD: Well, tell 'em to stop groanin'. Dere's nothin' de matter wid dat moon. Trouble is so many angels is flyin' over dere on Saddy night. Dey git to beatin' dere wings when dey dancin' an' dat makes de heat. Tell dem dat from now on dancin' 'roun' de moon is sinnin'. Dey got to stop it. Dat'll cool off de moon.

[*He swings back and puts the paper on the desk. He leans back in the chair comfortably, his hands clasped behind his head.*] Is dere anythin' else you ought to remin' me of?

40

GABRIEL: De prayers, Lawd.

GOD: [*Puzzled, slowly swinging chair around again.*] De prayers?

GABRIEL: From mankind. You know, down on de earth.

GOD: Oh, yeh, de poor little earth. Bless my soul, I almos' forgot about dat. Mus' be three or four hund'ed years since I been down dere. I wasn't any too pleased wid dat job.

GABRIEL: [*Laughing.*] You know you don' make mistakes, Lawd.

GOD: [*Soberly, with introspective detachment.*] So dey tell me. [*He looks at* GA-BRIEL, *then through the window again.*] So dey tell me. I fin' I kin be displeased though, an' I was displeased wid de mankind I las' seen. Maybe I ought to go down dere agin—I need a little holiday.

GABRIEL: Might do you good, Lawd.

GOD: I think I will. I'll go down an' walk de earth agin an' see how dem poor humans is makin' out. What time is it, by de sun an' de stars?

GABRIEL: [*Glancing out of the window.*] Jest exactly half-past, Lawd. [GOD *is taking his hat and stick from the hat rack.*]

GOD: [*Opening the door.*] Well, take keer o' yo'self. I'll be back Saddy. [*He exits. The stage is darkened. The* CHOIR *begins "Dere's no Hidin'-Place,"*

Oh, dere's no hidin'-place down dere,
Oh, dere's no hidin'-place down dere,
Oh, I went to de rock to hide my face,
De rock cried out, "No hidin'-place,"
   Dere's no hidin'-place down dere—

Oh, de rock cried, "I'm burnin' too,"
Yes, de rock cried, "I'm burnin' too,"
Oh, de rock cried out, "I'm burnin' too,
I wanter git to Heaven jes' as well as you."
   Dere's no hidin'-place down dere—

Oh, de sinner-man, he gambled an' fell,
Oh, de sinner-man, he gambled an' fell,
Oh, de sinner-man gambled, he gambled an' fell,
He meant to go to Heb'n but he landed in Hell.
   Dere's no hidin'-place down dere.

and continues until the lights go up on the next scene.]

SCENE VII

GOD *is walking along a country road. He stops to listen. Church bells are heard in the distance.*

GOD: Dat's nice. Nice an' quiet. Dat's de way I like Sunday to be. [*The sound is broken by the shrill voice of a girl. It is* ZEBA *singing a "blues."*] Now, dat ain't so good. [GOD *resumes his walk and the upper treadmill brings on a tree stump on which* ZEBA *is sitting. She is accompanying her song with a ukulele.* GOD *and the treadmills stop. When the stump reaches the center of the stage, it is seen that* ZEBA *is a rouged and extremely flashily dressed chippy of about eighteen.*] Stop dat!

ZEBA: What's de matter wid you, Country Boy? Pull up yo' pants. [*She resumes singing.*]

GOD: Stop dat!

ZEBA: [*Stops again.*] Say, listen to me, Banjo Eyes. What right you got to stop a lady enjoyin' herself?

GOD: Don't you know dis is de Sabbath? Da's no kin' o' song to sing on de Lawd's day.

ZEBA: Who care 'bout de Lawd's day, anymo'? People jest use Sunday now to git over Saddy.

GOD: You a awful sassy little girl.

ZEBA: I come fum sassy people! We even speak mean of de dead.

GOD: What's yo' name?

ZEBA: [*Flirtatiously.*] "What's my name?" Ain't you de ol'-time gal hunter! Fust, "What's my name?" den I s'pose, what would it be like if you tried to kiss me? You preachers is de debbils.

GOD: I ain't aimin' to touch you, daughter. [*A sudden sternness frightens* ZEBA. *She looks at him sharply.*] What is yo' name?

ZEBA: Zeba.

GOD: Who's yo' fam'ly?

ZEBA: I'm de great-great gran' daughter of Seth.

GOD: Of Seth? But Seth was a good man.

ZEBA: Yeh, he too good, he die of holiness.

GOD: An' yere's his little gran' daughter reekin' wid cologne. Ain't nobody ever tol' you yo' on de road to Hell?

ZEBA: [*Smiling.*] Sho' dat's what de preacher say. Exceptin' of course, I happens to know dat I'm on de road to de picnic groun's, an' at de present time I'm waitin' to keep a engagement wid my sweet papa. He don' like people talkin' to me. [CAIN THE SIXTH *enters. He is a young buck, wearing a "box" coat and the other flashy garments of a Rampart Street swell.*]

CAIN THE SIXTH: Hello, sugah! [*He crosses in front of* GOD *and faces* ZEBA.] Hello, mamma! Sorry I'm late baby, but de gals in de barrel-house jest wouldn't let me go. Doggone, one little wirehead swore she'd tear me down. [ZEBA *smiles and takes his hand.*]

GOD: What's yo' name, son?

CAIN THE SIXTH: [*Contemptuously; without turning.*] Soap 'n' water, Country Boy.

GOD: [*Sternly.*] What's yo' name, son? [CAIN *slowly turns and for a moment his manner is civil.*]

CAIN THE SIXTH: Cain the Sixth.

44

GOD: I was afraid so.

CAIN THE SIXTH: [*His impudence returning.*] You a new preacher?

GOD: Where you live?

CAIN THE SIXTH: Me, I live mos' any place.

GOD: Yes, an' you gonter see dem all. Is de udder young men all like you?

CAIN THE SIXTH: [*Smiling.*] De gals don' think so. [*He turns towards* ZEBA *again, picks her up and sits on the stump with the laughing* ZEBA *on his lap.*]

ZEBA: Dey ain't nobody in de worl' like my honey-cake. [CAIN *kisses her and she resumes her song.* GOD *watches them.* ZEBA *finishes a verse of the song and begins another softly.* CAIN THE SIXTH's *eyes have been closed during the singing.*]

CAIN THE SIXTH: [*His eyes closed.*] Is de preacher gone? [ZEBA *looks quickly at* GOD *without seeing him, and then looks off. She stops the song.*]

ZEBA: Yeh, I guess he walks fast. [CAIN *pushes her off his lap and rises.*]

CAIN THE SIXTH: [*With acid sweetness.*] Dey tell me las' night you was talkin' to a creeper man, baby.

ZEBA: Why, you know dey ain't nobody in de world fo' me but you.

CAIN THE SIXTH: [*Smiling.*] I know dey ain't. I even got dat guaranteed. [*Takes a revolver from his pocket.*] See dat, baby?

ZEBA: Sho' I see it, honey.

CAIN THE SIXTH: Dat jest makes me positive. [*Puts the gun back.*]

ZEBA: [*Pushing him back on the stump.*] You don' wanter believe dem stories, papa.

CAIN THE SIXTH: [*With sinister lightness.*] No, I didn't believe dem, baby. Co'se dat big gorilla, Flatfoot, from de other side of de river *is* in town ag'in.

ZEBA: Dat don' mean nothin'. Flatfoot ain't nothin' to me.

CAIN THE SIXTH: [*Sitting again.*] Co'se he ain't. Go 'head, sing some mo', baby. [ZEBA *resumes singing.*]

GOD: Bad business. [*The treadmills start turning.* GOD *resumes his walk.* ZEBA, *still singing, and* CAIN THE SIXTH *recede with the landscape.* GOD *is again alone*

45

on the country road. There is a twitter of birds. GOD looks up and smiles.] De birds is goin' 'bout dere business, all right. [A patch of flowers goes by, blackeyed Susans, conspicuously.] How you flowers makin' out? [Children's voices answer, "We O. K., Lawd."] Yes, an' you looks very pretty. [Children's voices: "Thank you, Lawd." The flowers pass out of sight.] It's only de human bein's makes me downhearted. Yere's as nice a Sunday as dey is turnin' out anywhere, an' nobody makin' de right use of it. [Something ahead of him attracts his attention. His face brightens.] Well, now dis is mo' like it. Now dat's nice to see people prayin'. It's a wonder dey don' do it in de church. But I fin' I don' min' it if dey do it outdoors. [A group of five adult Negroes and a boy on their knees in a semicircle, appears. The treadmills stop. The BOY, his head bent, swings his hands rhythmically up to his head three or four times. There is a hush.]

GAMBLER: Oh, Lawd, de smoke-house is empty. Oh, Lawd, lemme git dem groceries. Oh, Lawd, lemme see dat little *six*. [He casts the dice.] Wham! Dere she is, frien's. [Exclamations from the others, "Well damn my eyes!" "Doggone, dat's de eighth pass he make." "For God's sake, can't you ever crap?" etc. The BOY is picking up the money.]

GOD: Gamblin'! [Looks over the group's shoulders.] An' wid frozen dice!

BOY GAMBLER: Dey's a dolla' 'n' a half talkin' fo' me. How much you want of it, Riney?

FIRST GAMBLER: I take fo' bits. Wait a minute. Mebbe I take a little mo'. [He counts some money in his hand.]

SECOND GAMBLER: [Glancing up at GOD]. Hello, Liver Lips. [To the others.] Looka ol' Liver Lips. [The others look up and laugh good-naturedly, repeating "Liver Lips."]

FIRST GAMBLER: Ain't his pockets high from de groun'? Ol' High-Pockets. [The others keep saying "Ol' Liver Lips." "Ol' Liver Lips don't like to see people dicin'." Dat's a good name, 'High Pockets.'"]

BOY GAMBLER: [To others.] Come on, you gonter fade me or not? [GOD seizes the boy's ears and drags him to his feet. The others do not move, but watch, amused.]

46

GOD: Come yere, son. Why, yo' jest a little boy. Gamblin' an' sinnin'. [GOD *looks at the boy's face.*] You been chewin' tobacco, too, like you was yo' daddy. [GOD *sniffs.*] An' you been drinkin' sonny-kick-mammy-wine. You oughta be shamed. [*To the others.*] An' you gamblers oughta be 'shamed, leadin' dis boy to sin.

FIRST GAMBLER: He de bes' crap shooter in town, mister.

GOD. I'm gonter tell his mammy. I bet she don' know 'bout dis.

FIRST GAMBLER: No, she don' know. [*The others laugh.*] She don' know anythin'.

SECOND GAMBLER: Das de God's truth.

FIRST GAMBLER: See kin you beat 'im, High Pockets. Dey's a dolla' open yere.

GOD: I ain't gonter beat 'im. I'm gonter teach 'im. I may have to teach you all. [*He starts walking from them. The* BOY *sticks out his tongue the moment* GOD'S *back is turned.*]

BOY GAMBLER: If you fin' my mammy you do mo'n I kin. Come on, gamblers, see kin you gimme a little action. Who wants any part of dat dollar? [*The treadmill carries them off. The* FIRST GAMBLER *is heard saying,* "*I'll take anoder two bits,*" *and the others,* "*Gimme a dime's wo'th,*" "*I ain't only got fifteen cents left,*" *etc. as they disappear.*]

GOD: [*Walking.*] Where's dat little boy's home? [*The front of a shanty appears and* GOD *stops in front of the door.*] Yere's de place. It ain't any too clean, either. [*Knocks on the door with his cane.*]

VOICE IN SHANTY: Who dar?

GOD: Never you min' who's yere. Open de door.

VOICE IN SHANTY: You gotta search warrant?

GOD: I don' need one.

VOICE IN SHANTY: Who you wanter see?

GOD: I wanter see de mammy of de little gamblin' boy.

VOICE IN SHANTY: You mean little Johnny Rucker?

GOD: Dat may be his name.

VOICE IN SHANTY: Well, Mrs. Rucker ain't home.

GOD: Where's she at?

VOICE IN SHANTY: Who, Mrs. Rucker?

GOD: You heerd me.

VOICE IN SHANTY: Oh, she run away las' night wid a railroad man. She's *e*loped.

GOD: Where's Rucker?

VOICE IN SHANTY: He's flat under de table. He so drunk he cain't move.

GOD: Who are you?

VOICE IN SHANTY: I'se jest a fren' an' neighbor. I come in las' night to de party, an' everybody in yere's dead drunk but me. De only reason I kin talk is I drank some new white mule I made myself, an' it burn my throat so I cain't drink no mo'. You got any mo' questions?

GOD: Not for you. [*The shanty begins to move off as* GOD *starts walking again.*]

VOICE IN SHANTY: Good riddance, I say. [*Shanty disappears.*]

GOD: Dis ain't gittin' me nowheres. All I gotta say dis yere mankind I been peoplin' my earth wid sho' ain't much. [*He stops and looks back.*] I got good min' to wipe 'em all off an' people de earth wid angels. No. Angels is all right, singin' an' playin' an' flyin' around, but dey ain't much on workin' de crops and buildin' de levees. No, suh, mankind's jest right for my earth, if he wasn't so doggone sinful. I'd rather have my earth peopled wit' a bunch of channel catfish, dan I would mankin' an' his sin. I jest cain't stan' sin. [*He is about to resume his walk when* NOAH *enters.* NOAH *is dressed like a country preacher. His coat is of the "hammer-tail" variety. He carries a prayer book under his arm.*]

NOAH: Mo'nin', brother.

GOD: Mo'nin', brother. I declare you look like a good man.

NOAH: I try to be, brother. I'm de preacher yere. I don't think I seen you to de meetin'. [*They resume walking.*]

48

GOD: I jest come to town a little while ago an' I been pretty busy.

NOAH: Yes, mos' everybody say dey's pretty busy dese days. Dey so busy dey cain't come to meetin'. It seem like de mo' I preaches de mo' people ain't got time to come to church. I ain't hardly got enough members to fill up de choir. I gotta do de preachin' an' de bassin' too.

GOD: Is dat a fac'?

NOAH: Yes, suh, brother. Everybody is mighty busy, gamblin', good-timin', an' goin' on. You jest wait, though. When Gabriel blow de horn you gonter fin' dey got plenty of time to punch chunks down in Hell. Yes, suh.

GOD: Seems a pity. Dey all perfec'ly healthy?

NOAH: Oh, dey healthy, all right. Dey jest all lazy, and mean, and full of sin. You look like a preacher, too, brother.

GOD: Well, I am, in a way.

NOAH: You jest passin' through de neighborhood?

GOD: Yes. I wanted to see how things was goin' in yo' part of de country, an' I been feelin' jest 'bout de way you do. It's enough to discourage you.

NOAH: Yes, but I gotta keep wres'lin' wid 'em. Where you boun' for right now, brother?

GOD: I was jest walkin' along. I thought I might stroll on to de nex' town.

NOAH: Well, dat's a pretty good distance. I live right yere. [*He stops walking.*] Why don' you stop an' give us de pleasure of yo' comp'ny for dinner? I believe my ol' woman has kilt a chicken.

GOD: Why, dat's mighty nice of you, brother. I don' believe I caught yo' name.

NOAH: Noah, jest brother Noah. Dis is my home, brother. Come right in. [GOD *and* NOAH *start walking towards Noah's house which is just coming into view on the treadmill.*]

[The stage darkens, the CHOIR *sings "Some o' Dese Days,"*

Oh, I'm gonna set down at de welcome table,
Yes, I'm gonna set down at de welcome table
Some o' dese days, Hallelujah!
I'm gonna set down at de welcome table,
I'm-a gonna set down at de welcome table
   Some o' dese days.

Oh, I'm gonna feast on milk an' honey,
Yes, I'm gonna feast on milk an' honey
Some o' dese days, Hallelujah!
I'm gonna feast on milk an' honey,
I'm-a gonna feast on milk an' honey
   Some o' dese days.

Oh, I'm gonna drink from de Golden Fountain,
Yes, I'm gonna drink from de Golden Fountain
Some o' dese days, Hallelujah!
I'm gonna drink from de Golden Fountain,
I'm-a gonna drink from de Golden Fountain
   Some o' dese days.

and when the lights go up again, the next scene is disclosed.]

SCENE VIII

Interior of Noah's house. The ensemble suggests the combination living-dining room in a fairly prosperous Negro's cabin. Clean white curtains hang at the window. A table and chairs are in the center of the room. There is a cheerful checked tablecloth on the table, and on the wall, a framed, highly colored picture reading "God Bless Our Home." NOAH'S WIFE, *an elderly Negress, simply and neatly dressed,* GOD *and* NOAH *are discovered grouped about the table.*

NOAH: Company, darlin'. [*Noah's wife takes Noah's and God's hats.*] Dis gemman's a preacher, too. He's jest passin' through de country.

GOD: Good mo'nin', sister.

NOAH'S WIFE: Good mo'nin'. You jest ketch me when I'm gittin' dinner ready. You gonter stay with us?

GOD: If I ain't intrudin'. Brother Noah suggested—

NOAH'S WIFE: You set right down yere. I got a chicken in de pot an' it'll be ready in 'bout five minutes. I'll go out de back an' call Shem, Ham 'n' Japheth. [*To* GOD.] Dey's our sons. Dey live right acrost de way but always have Sunday dinner wid us. You mens make yo'selves comf'table.

51

GOD: Thank you, thank you very kindly.

NOAH: You run along, we all right. [GOD *and* NOAH *seat themselves.* NOAH'S WIFE *exits.*]

GOD: You got a fine wife, Brother Noah.

NOAH: She pretty good woman.

GOD: Yes, suh, an' you got a nice little home. Have a ten cent seegar? [GOD *offers him one.*]

NOAH: Thank you, much obliged. [*Both men lean back restfully in their chairs.*]

GOD: Jest what seems to be de main trouble 'mong mankind, Noah?

NOAH: Well, it seems to me de main trouble is dat de whol' distric' is wide open. Now you know dat makes fo' loose livin'. Men folks spen's all dere time fightin', loafin' an' gamblin', an' makin' bad likker.

GOD: What about de women?

NOAH: De women is worse dan de men. If dey ain't makin' love powder dey out beg, borrow an' stealin' money for policy tickets. Doggone, I come in de church Sunday 'fo' las' 'bout an' hour befo' de meetin' was to start, and dere was a woman stealin' de altar cloth. She was goin' to hock it. Dey ain't got no moral sense. Now you take dat case las' month, over in East Putney. Case of dat young Willy Roback.

GOD: What about him?

NOAH: Dere is a boy sebenteen years old. Doggone, if he didn't elope with his aunt. Now, you know, dat kin' of goin' on is bad fo' a neighborhood.

GOD: Terrible, terrible.

NOAH: Yes, suh. Dis use' to be a nice, decent community. I been doin' my best to preach de Word, but seems like every time I preach de place jest goes a little mo' to de dogs. De good Lawd only knows what's gonter happen.

GOD: Dat is de truth. [*There is a pause. Each puffs his cigar. Suddenly* NOAH *grasps his knee, as if it were paining him, and twists his foot.*]

NOAH: Huh!

GOD: What's de matter?

52

NOAH: I jest got a twitch. My buck-aguer I guess. Every now and den I gets a twitch in de knee. Might be a sign of rain.

GOD: That's just what it is. Noah, what's de mos' rain you ever had 'round dese parts?

NOAH: Well, de water come down fo' six days steady last April an' de ribber got so swole it bust down de levee up 'bove Freeport. Raise cain all de way down to de delta.

GOD: What would you say was it to rain for forty days and forty nights?

NOAH: I'd say dat was a *complete* rain!

GOD: Noah, you don't know who I is, do you?

NOAH: [*Puzzled.*] Yo' face looks easy, but I don' think I recall de name. [GOD *rises slowly, and as he reaches his full height there is a crash of lightning, a moment's darkness, and a roll of thunder. It grows light again.* NOAH *is on his knees in front of* GOD.] I should have known you. I should have seen de glory.

GOD: Dat's all right, Noah. You didn' know who I was.

NOAH: I'm jes' ol' preacher Noah, Lawd, an' I'm yo' servant. I ain' very much, but I'se all I got.

GOD: Sit down, Noah. Don' let me hear you shamin' yo'se'f, caize yo' a good man. [*Timidly* NOAH *waits until* GOD *is seated, and then sits, himself.*] I jest wanted to fin' out if you was good, Noah. Dat's why I'm walkin' de earth in de shape of a natchel man. I wish dey was mo' people like you. But, far as I kin see you and yo' fam'ly is de only respectable people in de worl'.

NOAH: Dey jest all poor sinners, Lawd.

GOD: I know. I am your Lawd. I am a god of wrath and vengeance an' dat's why I'm gonter destroy dis worl'.

NOAH: [*Almost in a whisper. Drawing back.*] Jest as you say, Lawd.

GOD: I ain't gonter destroy you, Noah. You and yo' fam'ly, yo' sheep an' cattle, an' all de udder things dat ain't human I'm gonter preserve. But de rest is gotta go. [*Takes a pencil and a sheet of paper from his pocket.*] Look yere, Noah. [NOAH *comes over and looks over his shoulder.*] I want you to build me a

55

boat. I want you to call it de "Ark," and I want it to look like dis. [*He is draw-ing on the paper. Continues to write as he speaks.*] I want you to take two of every kind of animal and bird dat's in de country. I want you to take seeds an' sprouts an' everythin' like dat an' put dem on dat Ark, because dere is gonter be all dat rain. Dey's gonter to be a deluge, Noah, an' dey's goin' to be a flood. De levees is gonter bust an' everything dat's fastened down is comin' loose, but it ain't gonter float long, caize I'm gonter make a storm dat'll sink everythin' from a hencoop to a barn. Dey ain't a ship on de sea dat'll be able to fight dat tempest. Dey all got to go. Everythin'. Everythin' in dis pretty worl' I made, except one thing, Noah. You an' yo' fam'ly an' de things I said are going to ride dat storm in de Ark. Yere's de way it's to be. [*He hands* NOAH *the paper.* NOAH *takes it and reads.*]

NOAH: [*Pause. Looks at paper again.*] Yes, suh, dis seems to be complete. Now 'bout the animals, Lawd, you say you want everythin'?

GOD: Two of everythin'.

NOAH: Dat would include jayraffes an' hippopotamusses?

GOD: Everythin' dat is.

NOAH: Dey was a circus in town las' week. I guess I kin fin' dem. Co'se I kin git all de rabbits an' possums an' wil' turkeys easy. I'll sen' de boys out. Hum, I'm jest wonderin'—

GOD: 'Bout what?

NOAH: 'Bout snakes? Think you'd like snakes, too?

GOD: Certainly, I want snakes.

NOAH: Oh, I kin git snakes, lots of 'em. Co'se, some of 'em's a little dan-gerous. Maybe I better take a kag of likker, too?

GOD: You kin have a kag of likker.

NOAH: [*Musingly.*] Yes, suh, dey's a awful lot of differ'nt kin's of snakes, come to think about it. Dey's water moccasins, cotton-moufs, rattlers—mus' be a hund'ed kin's of other snakes down in de swamps. Maybe I better take two kags of likker.

56

GOD: [*Mildly.*] I think de one kag's enough.

NOAH: No. I better take two kags. Besides I kin put one on each side of de boat, an' balance de ship wid dem as well as havin' dem fo' medicinal use.

GOD: You kin put one kag in de middle of de ship.

NOAH: [*Buoyantly.*] Jest as easy to take de two kags, Lawd.

GOD: I think one kag's enough.

NOAH: Yes, Lawd, but you see forty days an' forty nights—[*There is a distant roll of thunder.*]

GOD: [*Firmly.*] One kag, Noah.

NOAH: Yes, Lawd. One kag. [*The door in the back opens and* NOAH'S WIFE *enters with a tray of dishes and food.*]

NOAH'S WIFE: Now, den, gen'lemen, if you'll jest draw up cheers. [*The stage is darkened. The* CHOIR *is heard singing "I Wanter Be Ready."*

I wanter be ready,
I wanter be ready,
I wanter be ready, my Lord,
To walk in Jerusalem
   Jes' like John.

John said dat city was jes' fo'-square,
   Walk in Jerusalem jes' like John
An' he declared he'd meet me there.
   Walk in Jerusalem jes' like John.

I wanter be ready,
I wanter be ready,
I wanter be ready, my Lord,
To walk in Jerusalem
   Jes' like John.

I wanter be ready,
I wanter be ready,
I wanter be ready, my Lord,
To walk in Jerusalem
　Jes' like John.

They continue in the darkness until the lights go up on the next scene.]

SCENE IX

In the middle of the stage is the Ark. On the hillside, below the Ark, a dozen or more men and women, townspeople, are watching NOAH, SHEM, HAM *and* JAPHETH *on the deck of the Ark. The three sons are busily nailing boards on the cabin.* NOAH *is smoking a pipe. He wears a silk hat, captain's uniform and a "slicker."*

NOAH: [*To* SHEM.] You, Shem, tote up some ol' rough lumber, don' bring up any planed up lumber, caize dat ain't fo' de main deck.

SHEM: Pretty near supper time, daddy.

NOAH: Maybe 'tis, but I got de feelin' we ought to keep goin'.

FIRST WOMAN: You gonter work all night, Noah, maybe, huh?

NOAH: [*Without looking at her.*] If de sperrit move me.

SECOND WOMAN: Look yere, Noah, whyn't you give up all dis damn foolishness? Don' you know people sayin' yo' crazy? What you think you doin' anyway?

NOAH: I'se buildin' a Ark. [*Other men and women join those in the foreground.*] Ham, you better stop for a while 'n' see whether dey bringin' de animals up all right. [*He looks at his watch.*] Dey ought to be pretty near de foot o' de hill by dis time; if dey ain't you wait fo' dem and bring 'em yo'se'f. [HAM *goes down a lad-*

59

der at the side of the ship and exits during the following scene. The newcomers in group have been speaking to some of the early arrivals.]

SECOND WOMAN: [*To* THIRD WOMAN, *one of the newcomers.*] No, you don't mean it!

THIRD WOMAN: I do so. Dat's what de talk is in de town.

FIRST MAN: You hear dat, Noah? Dey say yo' ol' lady is tellin' everybody it's gonter rain fo' fo'ty days and fo'ty nights. You know people soon gonter git de idea you *all* crazy.

NOAH: Lot I keer what you think. [*To* JAPHETH.] Straighten up dem boards down dere, Japheth. [*Indicates floor of deck.*]

FIRST MAN: [*To* THIRD WOMAN.] Was I you, I wouldn' go 'round with Mrs. Noah anymore, lady. Fust thing you know you'll be gittin' a hard name, too.

THIRD WOMAN: Don' I know?

SECOND WOMAN: A lady cain't be too partic'lar dese days. [ZEBA *and* FLATFOOT, *a tall, black, wicked-looking buck, enter, their arms around each other's waist.*]

ZEBA: Dere it is, baby. Was I lyin'?

FLATFOOT: Well, I'll be split in two!

FIRST MAN: What you think of it, Flatfoot?

FLATFOOT: I must say! Look like a house wit' a warpin' cellar.

NOAH: Dis yere vessel is a boat.

FLATFOOT: When I was a little boy dey used to build boats down near de ribber, where de water was. [*The others laugh.*]

NOAH: Dis time it's been arranged to have de water come up to de boat. [JAPHETH *looks belligerently over the rail of the Ark at* FLATFOOT. *To* JAPHETH.] Keep yo' shirt on, son.

SECOND WOMAN: [*To* THIRD WOMAN.] Now, you see de whole fam'ly's crazy.

THIRD WOMAN: Listen, dey ain't gonter 'taminate me. It was me dat started resolvin' dem both out o' de buryin' society.

60

ZEBA: When all dis water due up yere, Noah?

NOAH: You won't know when it gits yere, daughter.

ZEBA: Is she goin' to be a side-wheeler, like de Bessy-Belle?

FLATFOOT: No! If she was a side-wheeler she'd get her wheels all clogged wid sharks. She gonter have jus' one great big stern wheel, like de Commodore. Den if dey ain't 'nuf water why de big wheel kin stir some up. [*General laughter. Two or three of the* GAMBLERS *enter and join the group, followed by* CAIN THE SIXTH.]

CAIN THE SIXTH: Dere's de fool an' his monument, jest like I said! [*The* GAMBLERS *and* CAIN THE SIXTH *roar with laughter, slap their legs, etc., the members of the main group talk sotto voce to each other as* CAIN THE SIXTH *catches* ZEBA'S *eye.* FLATFOOT *is on her right and is not aware of* CAIN THE SIXTH'S *presence.*]

NOAH: See how dey makin' out inside, son. [*Stops hammering.* JAPHETH *exits into Ark.* NOAH *turns and gazes towards the east.*]

CAIN THE SIXTH: Hello, honey.

ZEBA: [*Frightened but smiling.*] Hello, sugah.

CAIN THE SIXTH: [*Pleasantly.*] Ain't dat my ol' frien' Flatfoot wid you?

ZEBA: Why, so 'tis! [FLATFOOT *is now listening. To* FLATFOOT.] He's got a gun.

CAIN THE SIXTH: No, I ain't. [*He lifts his hands over his head.* ZEBA *quickly advances and runs her hands lightly over his pockets.*]

ZEBA: [*Relieved.*] I guess he ain't.

CAIN THE SIXTH: No, I ain't got no gun for my ol' friend, Flatfoot. [*He walks up to him.*]

FLATFOOT: [*Smiling.*] Hi, Cain. How's de boy? [CAIN *quickly presses his chest against* FLATFOOT'S, *his downstage arm sweeps around* FLATFOOT'S *body and his hand goes up to the small of* FLATFOOT'S *back.*]

CAIN THE SIXTH: [*Quietly, but triumphantly.*] I got a little *knife* fo' *him.* [FLATFOOT *falls dead. The laughter of the others stops and they look at the scene.* ZEBA *for a moment is terrified, her clenched hand pressed to her mouth. She looks at* CAIN THE SIXTH, *who is smiling at her. He tosses the knife on the ground and holds his hands out to her. She goes to him, smiling.*]

ZEBA: You sho' take keer of me, honey.

CAIN THE SIXTH: Dat's caize I think yo' wo'th takin' keer of. [*To the others.*] It's all right, folks. I jest had to do a little cleanin' up.

FIRST WOMAN: [*Smiling.*] You is de quickes' scoundrel.

FIRST GAMBLER: It was a nice quick killin'. Who was he?

SECOND WOMAN: [*Casually.*] Dey called him Flatfoot. From over de river. He wa'nt any good. He owed me for washin' for over a year.

THIRD WOMAN: Used to peddle muggles. Said it had a kick like reg'lar snow. Wasn't no good.

SECOND GAMBLER: Think we ought to bury him?

FIRST MAN: No, just leave him dere. Nobody comes up yere, 'cept ol' Manatee. [*Indicates* NOAH. *Cries of "Ol' Manatee! Ol' Manatee, dat's good!"*]

NOAH: [*Still looking off.*] You bettah pray, you po' chillun. [*They all laugh.*]

FIRST WOMAN: We bettah pray? You bettah pray, Ol' Manatee.

ZEBA: You bettah pray for rain. [*Laughter again.*]

NOAH: Dat's what I ain't doin', sinners. Shem! Japheth! [*To others, as he points off. Patter of rain.*] Listen!

CAIN THE SIXTH: [*Casually.*] Doggone, I believe it *is* gonter shower a little.

FIRST GAMBLER: It do looks like rain.

FIRST WOMAN: I think I'll git on home. I got a new dress on.

ZEBA: Me, too. I wants to keep lookin' nice fo' my sweet papa. [*She pats* CAIN THE SIXTH'S *cheek.* CAIN THE SIXTH *hugs her.*]

NOAH: [*Almost frantically.*] Ham! Is de animals dere?

HAM: [*Off stage.*] Yes, sir, dere yere. We're comin'.

NOAH: Den bring 'em on. [SHEM *and* JAPHETH *come on deck with their hammers.*]

THIRD WOMAN: I guess we all might go home 'til de shower's over. Come on, papa.

SECOND GAMBLER: See you after supper, Noah. [*Crowd starts moving off right.*]

62

NOAH: God's gittin' ready to start, my sons. Let's git dis plankin' done.

ZEBA: Put a bix Texas on it, Noah, an' we'll use it fo' excursions. [*There is a distant roll of thunder, there are cries of "Good night, Admiral." "See you later." "So long, Manatee," as the crowd goes off. The thunder rumbles again. There is the sound of increasing rain. The hammers of* SHEM *and* JAPHETH *sound louder and are joined by the sounds of other hammerers. There is a flash of lightning. The sounds on the Ark become faster and louder. The rush of rain grows heavier.*]

NOAH: Hurry! Hurry! Where are you, Ham?

HAM: [*Just off stage.*] Yere, I am, father, wid de animals.

NOAH: God's give us his sign. Send 'em up de gangplank. [*An inclined plane is thrown against the Ark from the side of the stage by* HAM, *who cracks a whip.*]

HAM: Get on, dere. [*The heads of two elephants are seen.*]

NOAH: Bring 'em on board! De Lawd is strikin' down de worl'! [*The* CHOIR *begins singing "Ol' Ark's A-Moverin'." The singing and the noises reach fortissimo as* HAM *cracks his whip again, and the rain falls on the stage. The stage is darkened. The* CHOIR *continues singing in the darkness.*]

> Oh, de ol' Ark's a-moverin',
> Moverin', moverin',
> De ol' Ark's a-moverin',
> Moverin' along.
>
> Oh, de ol' Ark's a-moverin',
> Moverin', moverin',
> De ol' Ark's a-moverin',
> Moverin' along.
>
> Wait a little while I'm gonna tell yer 'bout de ol' ark,
> Ol' Ark's a-moverin', moverin' along.
> God tol' Noah fer ter buil' Him a ol' ark,
> Ol' Ark's a-moverin', moverin' along.

Oh, de ol' Ark's a-moverin',
Moverin', moverin',
De ol' Ark's a-moverin',
Moverin' along.

Oh, de ol' Ark's a-moverin',
Moverin', moverin',
De ol' Ark's a-moverin',
Moverin' along.

Ol' Ark she reel,
Ol' Ark she rock,
Ol' Ark she landed
On de mountain top.

Oh, de ol' Ark's a-moverin',
Moverin', moverin',
De ol' Ark's a-moverin',
Moverin' along.

Oh, de ol' Ark's a-moverin',
Moverin', moverin',
De ol' Ark's a-moverin',
Moverin' along.

SCENE X

When the lights go up on scene, the Ark is at sea. Stationary waves run in front of it. The hillside has disappeared. The Ark is in the only lighted area. SHEM *is smoking a pipe on the deck, leaning on the rail. A steamboat whistle blows three short and one long blast.* SHEM *is surprised. In a moment* HAM *appears, also with a pipe, and joins* SHEM *at the rail.*

SHEM: Who'd you think you was signallin'?

HAM: Dat wasn't me, dat was daddy.

SHEM: He think he gonter git a reeply?

HAM: I don' know. He's been gittin' a heap of comfort out of dat likker.

SHEM: De kag's nearly empty, ain't it?

HAM: Pretty nearly almos'. [*They look over the rail. A pause.*] Seen anythin'?

SHEM: Dis mornin' I seen somethin' over dere migh'a' been a fish.

HAM: Dat's de big news of de week.

SHEM: How long you think dis trip's gonter las'?

HAM: I don' know! Rain fo'ty days 'n' fo'ty nights an' when dat stop' I thought sho' we'd come up ag'inst a san' bar o' somethin'. Looks now like all

67

dat rain was jest a little incident of de trip. [*The whistle blows again.*] Doggone! I wish he wouldn't do dat. Fust thing we know he'll wake up dem animals ag'in. [JAPHETH *appears.*]

SHEM: What de matter wit' de ol' man, Jape?

JAPHETH: Doggone, he say he had a dream dat we're nearly dere. Dat's why he pullin' de whistle cord. See kin he git a' answer. [*He looks over the rail.*] Look to me like de same ol' territory. [MRS. NOAH *appears on deck.*]

NOAH'S WIFE: You boys go stop yo' paw pullin' dat cord. He so full of likker he think he's in a race.

JAPHETH: He claim he know what he's doin'.

NOAH'S WIFE: I claim he gittin' to be a perfec' nuisance. Me an' yo' wives cain't hardly heah ou'sel'es think. [NOAH *appears, his hat rakishly tilted on his head. He goes to the railing and looks out.*] You 'spectin' company?

NOAH: Leave me be, woman. De watah don' look so rough today. De ol' boat's ridin' easier.

NOAH'S WIFE: Ridin' like a ol' mule!

NOAH: Yes, suh, de air don't feel so wet. Shem! 'Spose you sen' out 'nother dove. [SHEM *goes into the Ark.*] Ham, go git de soundin' line. Jape, keep yo' eye on de East. [JAPHETH *goes to the end of the boat.*]

NOAH'S WIFE: As fo' you, I s'pose you'll help things along by takin' a little drink.

NOAH: Look yere, who's de pilot of dis vessel?

NOAH'S WIFE: Ol' Mister Dumb Luck.

NOAH: Well, see dat's where you don' know anythin'.

NOAH'S WIFE: I s'pose you ain't drunk as a fool?

NOAH: [*Cordially.*] I feel congenial.

NOAH'S WIFE: An' you look it. You look jest wonderful. I wonder if you'd feel so congenial if de Lawd was to show up?

NOAH: De Lawd knows what I'm doin', don' you worry 'bout dat.

NOAH'S WIFE: I wouldn't say anythin' ag'inst de Lawd. He suttinly let

68

us know dey'd be a change in de weather. But I bet even de Lawd wonders sometimes why he ever put you in charge.

NOAH: Well, you let de Lawd worry 'bout dat. [SHEM *appears with the dove.*]

SHEM: Will I leave her go, Paw?

NOAH: Leave 'er go.

[*There is a chorus of "Good Luck, Dove," from the group as the dove flies off stage.* HAM *appears with the sounding line.*] Throw 'er over, Boy. [HAM *proceeds to do so.*]

NOAH'S WIFE: An' another thing—

HAM: Hey!

NOAH: [*Rushing to his side.*] What is it?

HAM: Only 'bout a inch! Look! [*They lean over.*]

JAPHETH: It's gettin' light in de East. [*As* HAM *works the cord up and down,* NOAH *and* NOAH'S WIFE *turn toward* JAPHETH. *The* CHOIR *begins "My Soul Is a Witness for the Lord."*]

My soul is a witness	You read in de Bible, you understan'
For my Lord,	Dat Noah was a righteous man.
My soul is a witness	De Lord appeared to him in de dark
For my Lord.	Commanded him for to buil' de Ark.
My soul is a witness	Oh, Noah was a witness
For my Lord,	For my Lord,
My soul is a witness	Noah was a witness
For my Lord.	For my Lord.

NOAH: Praise de Lawd, so it is.

NOAH'S WIFE: Oh, dat's pretty.

NOAH: [*To* HAM.] An' de boat's stopped. We've landed. Shem, go down 'n' drag de fires an' dreen de boiler. Yo go help 'im, Ham.

JAPHETH: Look, Paw. [*The dove wings back to the Ark with an olive branch in its mouth.*]

NOAH: 'N' yere's de little dove wid greenery in its mouth! Take 'er down, Jape, so she kin tell de animals. [JAPHETH *exits after* SHEM *and* HAM *carrying the dove. To* MRS. NOAH.] Now, maybe you feel little different.

NOAH'S WIFE: [*Contritely.*] It was jes' gittin' to be so tiresome. I'm sorry, Noah.

NOAH: Dat's all right, ol' woman. [NOAH'S WIFE *exits.* NOAH *looks about him. The lights have changed and the water piece is gone and the Ark is again on the hillside. Two mountains can be seen in the distance and a rainbow slowly appears over the Ark. The singing has grown louder.*] Thank you, Lawd, thank you very much indeed. Amen. [*The singing stops with the "Amen."* GOD *appears on the deck.*]

GOD: Yo' welcome, Noah. [NOAH *turns and sees him.*]

NOAH: O, Lawd, it's wonderful.

GOD: [*Looking about him.*] I sort of like it. I like de way you handled de ship, too, Noah.

NOAH: Was you watchin', Lawd?

GOD: Every minute. [*He smiles.*] Didn't de ol' lady light into you?

NOAH: [*Apologetically.*] She was kinda restless.

GOD: That's all right. I ain't blamin' nobody. I don' even min' you' cussin' an' drinkin'. I figure a steamboat cap'n on a long trip like you had has a right to a little redeye, jest so he don' go crazy.

NOAH: Thank you, Lawd. What's de orders now?

GOD: All de animals safe?

NOAH: Dey all fin'n' dandy, Lawd.

GOD: Den I want you to open dat starboard door, an' leave 'em all out. Let 'em go down de hill. Den you an' de family take all de seeds 'n'de sprouts an' begin plantin' ag'in. I'm startin' all over, Noah. [NOAH *exits.* GOD *looks around.*]

GOD: Well, now we'll see what happens. [GOD *listens with a smile, as noises accompanying the debarking of the animals are heard. There are the cracks of whips, the voices of the men on the Ark, shouting: "Git along dere." "Whoa, take it easy." "Duck*

70

yo' head." "Keep in line, dere," etc. *Over the Ark there is a burst of centrifugal shadows, and the sound of a myriad of wings.* GOD *smiles at the shadows.*] Dat's right, birds, fin' yo' new homes. [*Bird twitters are heard again.* GOD *listens a moment and rests an arm on the railing. He speaks softly.*] Gabriel, kin you spare a minute? [GABRIEL *appears.*]

GABRIEL: Yes, Lawd. [*The sounds from the other side of the Ark are by now almost hushed. The* LORD *indicates the new world with a wave of the hand.*]

GOD: Well, it's did.

GABRIEL: [*Respectfully, but with no enthusiasm.*] So I take notice.

GOD: Yes, suh, startin' all over again.

GABRIEL: So I see.

GOD: [*Looking at him suddenly.*] Don' seem to set you up much.

GABRIEL: Well, Lawd, you see—[*He hesitates.*] 'Tain't none of my business.

GOD: What?

GABRIEL: I say, I don' know very much about it.

GOD: I know you don'. I jest wanted you to see it. [*A thought strikes him.*] Co'se, it ain' yo' business, Gabe. It's my business. 'Twas my idea. De whole thing was my idea. An' every bit of it's my business 'n nobody else's. De whole thing rests on my shoulders. I declare, I guess *dat's* why I feel so solemn and serious, at dis particklar time. You know *dis* thing's turned into quite a proposition.

GABRIEL: [*Tenderly.*] But, it's all right, Lawd, as you say, it's did.

GOD: Yes, suh, it's did. [*Sighs deeply. Looks slowly to the right and the left. Then softly.*] I only hope it's goin' to work out all right.

CURTAIN

I am a po' pilgrim of sorrow,
I'm tossed in dis wide worl' alone;
No hope have I for tomorrow,
I've started to make Heav'n my home.

Sometimes I am tossted an' driven, Lord,
Sometimes I don' know where to roam.
I heard of a city called Heaven,
I've started to make it my home.

My mother has reached dat pure glory,
My father's still walkin' in sin;
My brothers an' sisters won't own me
Because I am try'n' to get in.

Sometimes I am tossted an' driven, Lord,
Sometimes I don' know where to roam.
I heard of a city called Heaven,
I've started to make it my home.

Sometimes I am tossted an' driven, Lord,
Sometimes I don' know where to roam.
I heard of a city called Heaven,
I've started to make it my home.

THE

GREEN

PASTURES

PART TWO

PART TWO

SCENE I

GOD'S *office again. Somewhere the* CHOIR *is singing, "A City Called Heaven." In the office are* TWO WOMEN CLEANERS. *One is scrubbing the floor, the other dusting the furniture. The one dusting stops and looks out the window. There is a whirr and a distant faint boom. The* CHOIR *stops.*

FIRST CLEANER: Dat was a long way off.

SECOND CLEANER: [*At window.*] Yes, ma'am. An' dat must a' been a big one. Doggone, de Lawd mus' be mad fo' sho', dis mo'nin'. Dat's de fo'ty-six' thunde'-bolt since breakfast.

FIRST CLEANER: I wonder where at He's pitchin' dem.

SECOND CLEANER: My goodness, don' you know?

FIRST CLEANER: [*A little hurt.*] Did I know I wouldn't ask de question.

SECOND CLEANER: Every one of dem's bound fo' de earth.

FIRST CLEANER: De earth? You mean dat little ol' dreenin' place?

SECOND CLEANER: Dat's de planet. [*Another faint whirr and boom.*] Dere goes another.

79

FIRST CLEANER: Well, bless me. *I* didn't know dey was thunde'bolts.

SECOND CLEANER: Wha'd you think dey was?

FIRST CLEANER: [*Above desk.*] I wasn't sho', but I thought maybe He might be whittlin' a new star o' two, an' de noise was jest de chips fallin'.

SECOND CLEANER: Carrie, where you been? Don' you know de earth is de new scandal? Ever'body's talkin' 'bout it.

FIRST CLEANER: Dey kep' it from me.

SECOND CLEANER: Ain't you noticed de Lawd's been unhappy lately?

FIRST CLEANER: [*Thoughtfully.*] Yeah, He ain't been his old self.

SECOND CLEANER: What did you think was de matteh? Lumbago?

FIRST CLEANER: [*Petulantly.*] I didn't know. I didn't think it was fo' me t'inquieh.

SECOND CLEANER: Well, it jest so happens dat de Lawd is riled as kin be by that measly little earth. Or I should say de scum dat's on it.

FIRST CLEANER: Dat's mankind down dere.

SECOND CLEANER: Dey mus' be scum, too, to git de Lawd so wukked up.

FIRST CLEANER: I s'pose so. [*Another whirr and boom.*] Looks like He's lettin' dem feel de wrath. Ain' dat a shame to plague de Lawd dat way?

SECOND CLEANER: From what I hear dey been beggin' fo' what dey're gittin'. My brother flew down to bring up a saint de other day and he say from what he see mos' of de population down dere has made de debbil king an' dey wukkin' in three shifts fo' him.

FIRST CLEANER: You cain't blame de Lawd.

SECOND CLEANER: Co'se you cain't. Dem human bein's 'd make any-body bile oveh. Ev'rytime de Lawd try to do sompin' fo' dem, doggone if dey don't staht some new ruckus.

FIRST CLEANER: I take notice He's been wukkin' in yere mo' dan usual.

SECOND CLEANER: I wish He'd let us ladies fix it up. Wouldn't take a minute to make dis desk gold-plated.

80

FIRST CLEANER: I s'pose He likes it dis way. De Lawd's kind o' ol' fashioned in some ways. I s'pose He keeps dis office plain an' simple on purpose.

SECOND CLEANER: [*Finishing her work.*] I don' see why.

FIRST CLEANER: [*Looking off.*] Well, it's kind of a nice place to come to when He's studyin' somethin' impo'tant. 'Most evahthin' else in heaven's so fin' 'n' gran', maybe ev'ry now an den He jest gits sick an' tired of de glory. [*She is also collecting her utensils.*]

SECOND CLEANER: Maybe so. Jest de same I'd like to have a free hand wid dis place for a while, so's I could gold it up. [GOD *appears in the doorway.*]

GOD: Good mo'nin', daughters.

FIRST AND SECOND CLEANERS: Good mo'nin', Lawd. We was jest finishin'.

GOD: Go ahead den, daughters. [*Goes to the window.*]

FIRST AND SECOND CLEANERS: Yes, Lawd. [*They exeunt. Off stage.*] Good mo'nin', Gabriel. [*Off stage* GABRIEL *says, "Good mo'nin', sisters," and enters immediately. He stands in the doorway for a moment watching* GOD—*a note-book and pencil in his hand.*]

GOD: What's de total?

GABRIEL: [*Consulting the book.*] Eighteen thousand nine hund'ed an' sixty for de mo'nin'. Dat's includin' de village wid de fo'tune tellers. Dey certainly kin breed fast.

GOD: [*Solemnly.*] Dey displease me. Dey displease me greatly.

GABRIEL: Want some more bolts, Lawd?

GOD: [*Looking through window.*] Look at 'em dere. Squirmin' an' fightin' an' bearin' false witness. Listen to dat liar, dere. He don' intend to marry dat little gal. He don' even love her. What did you say?

GABRIEL: Should I git mo' bolts?

GOD: Wait a minute. [*He carefully points his finger down through the window.*] I'm goin' to git dat wicked man myself. [*From a great distance comes an agonized cry:*

"Oh, Lawd!" GOD *turns from the window.*] No use gittin' mo' thunde'bolts. Dey don' do de trick. [*He goes to the swivel chair and sits.*] It's got to be somethin'else.

GABRIEL: How would it be if you was to doom 'em all ag'in, like dat time you sent down de flood? I bet dat would make dem mind.

GOD: You see how much good de flood did. Dere dey is, jest as bad as ever.

GABRIEL: How about cleanin' up de whole mess of 'em and sta'tin' all over ag'in with some new kind of animal?

GOD: An' admit I'm licked?

GABRIEL: [*Ashamedly.*] No, of co'se not, Lawd.

GOD: No, suh. No, suh. Man is a kind of pet of mine and it ain't right fo' me to give up tryin' to do somethin' wid him. Doggone, mankin' *mus'* be all right at de core or else why did I ever bother wid him in de first place? [*Sits at desk.*]

GABRIEL: It's jest dat I hates to see you worryin' about it, Lawd.

GOD: Gabe, dere ain't anythin' worth while anywheres dat didn't 'cause somebody some worryin'. I ain't never tol' you de trouble I had gittin' things started up yere. Dat's a story in itself. No, suh, de more I keep on bein' de Lawd de more I know I got to keep improvin' things. An' dat takes time and worry. De main trouble with mankin' is he takes up so much of my time. He ought to be able to help hisself a little. [*He stops suddenly and cogitates.*] Hey, dere! I think I got it!

GABRIEL: [*Eagerly.*] What's de news?

GOD: [*Still cogitating.*] Yes, suh, dat seems like an awful good idea.

GABRIEL: Tell me, Lawd.

GOD: Gabriel, have you noticed dat every now an' den, mankin' turns out some pretty good specimens?

GABRIEL: Dat's de truth.

GOD: Yes, suh. Dey's ol' Abraham and Isaac an' Jacob an' all dat family.

GABRIEL: Dat's so, Lawd.

GOD: An' everyone of dem boys was a hard wukker an' a good citizen. We got to admit dat.

82

GABRIEL: Dey wouldn't be up yere flyin' wid us if dey hadn't been.

GOD: No, suh. An' I don' know but what de answer to de whole trouble is right dere.

GABRIEL: How you mean, Lawd?

GOD: Why, doggone it, de good man is de man dat keeps busy. I mean I been goin' along on de principle dat he was something like you angels—dat you ought to be able to give him somethin' an' den jest let him sit back an' enjoy it. Dat ain't so. Now dat I recollec' I put de first one down dere to take keer o' dat garden an' den I let him go ahead an' do nothin' but git into mischief. [*He rises.*] Sure, *dat's* it. He ain't *built* jest to fool 'roun' an' not do nothin'. Gabe, I'm gonter try a new scheme.

GARBIEL: [*Eagerly.*] What's de scheme, Lawd?

GOD: I'll tell you later. Send in Abraham, Isaac an' Jacob. [*A voice outside calls*: "*Right away, Lawd.*"] You go tell dem to put dem bolts back in de boxes. I ain' gonter use dem ag'in a while.

GABRIEL: O. K., Lawd.

GOD: Was you goin' anywhere near de Big Pit?

GABRIEL: I could go.

GOD: Lean over de brink and tell Satan he's jest a plain fool if he thinks he kin beat anybody as big as me.

GABRIEL: Yes, suh, Lawd. Den I'll spit right in his eye. [GABRIEL *exits.* GOD *looks down through the window again to the earth below.*]

GOD: Dat new polish on de sun makes it powerful hot. [*He "r'ars back."*] Let it be jest a little bit cooler. [*He feels the air.*] Dat's nice. [*Goes to His desk. A knock on the door.*] Come in. [ABRAHAM, ISAAC *and* JACOB *enter. All are very old men, but the beard of* ABRAHAM *is the longest and whitest, and they suggest their three generations. They have wings that are not quite so big as those of the native angels.*]

ISAAC: Sorry we so long comin', Lawd. But Pappy and me had to take de boy [*Pointing to* JACOB] over to git him a can of wing ointment.

GOD: What was de matter, son?

85

JACOB: Dey was chafin' me a little. Dey fine now, thank you, Lawd.

GOD: Dat's good. Sit down an' make yo'selves comf'table. [*The three sit.* MEN: *"Thank you, Lawd."*] Men, I'm goin' to talk about a little scheme I got. It's one dat's goin' to affec' yo' fam'lies an' dat's why I 'cided I'd talk it over wid you, 'fo' it goes into ee-fect. I don' know whether you boys know it or not, but you is about de three best men of one fam'ly dat's come up yere since I made little apples. Now I tell you what I'm gonter do. Seein' dat you human bein's cain't 'preciate anythin' lessen you fust wukk to git it and den keep strugglin' to hold it, why I'm gonter turn over a very valuable piece of property to yo' fam'ly, and den see what kin dey do with it. De rest of de worl' kin go jump in de river fo' all I keer. I'm gonter be lookin' out fo' yo' descendants only. Now den, seein' dat you boys know de country pretty tho'ly, where at does you think is de choice piece of property in de whole worl'? Think it over for a minute. I'm gonter let you make de s'lection.

ABRAHAM: If you was to ask me, Lawd, I don't think dey come any better dan de Land of Canaan.

GOD: [*To* ISAAC *and* JACOB.] What's yo' feelin' in de matter?

JACOB: [*After a nod from* ISAAC.] Pappy an' me think do we get a pick, dat would be it.

GOD: [*Goes to window again, looks out.*] De Land of Canaan. Yes, I guess dat's a likely neighborhood. It's all run over wid Philistines and things right now, but we kin clean dat up. [*He turns from the window and resumes his seat.*] All right. Now who do you boys think is de best of yo' men to put in charge down dere? You see I ain't been payin' much attention to anybody in partic'lar lately.

ISAAC: Does you want de brainiest or de holiest, Lawd? [MEN *look up.*]

GOD: I want de holiest. I'll make him brainy. [MEN *appreciate the miracle.*]

ISAAC: Well, if you want A Number One Goodness, Lawd, I don't know where you'll git more satisfaction dan in a great-great-great-great grandson of mine.

GOD: Where's he at?

86

ISAAC: At de moment I b'lieve he's in de sheep business over in Midian County. He got in a little trouble down in Egypt, but t'wan't his doin'. He killed a man dat was abusin' one of our boys in de brick works. Of co'se you know old King Pharaoh's got all our people in bondage.

GOD: I heard of it. [*With some ire.*] Who did you think put them dere? [*The visitors lower their heads.*] It's all right, boys. [*All rise.*] I'm gonter take dem out of it. An' I'm gonter turn over de whole Land of Canaan to dem. An' do you know whose gonter lead dem dere? Yo' great-great-great-great grandson. Moses, ain't it?

ISAAC: Yes, Lawd.

GOD: [*Smiling.*] Yes. I been noticin' *him*.

ABRAHAM: It's quite a favor fo' de fam'ly, Lawd.

GOD: Dat's why I tol' you. You see, it so happens I love yo' fam'ly, an' I delight to honor it. Dat's all, gen'lemen. [*The three others rise and cross to the door, murmuring, "Yes, Lawd," "Thank you, Lawd," "Much obliged, Lawd." etc.* GOD *stands watching the men leave.*] Enjoy yo' selves. [*He goes to the window. He speaks through the window to the earth.*] I'm comin' down to see you, Moses, an' dis time my scheme's *got* to wukk. [*The* CHOIR *begins "My Lord's A-Writin' All De Time."*

Oh, he sees all you do
An' he hears all you say,
    My Lord's a-writin' all de time.

Oh, he sees all you do
An' he hears all you say,
    My Lord's a-writin' all de time.

When I was down in de Egyp' lan',
    My Lord's a-writin' all de time.

87

I heard good news from de promise' lan',
  My Lord's a-writin' all de time.

Oh, he sees all you do
An' he hears all you say,
  My Lord's a-writin' all de time.

King Jesus rides in de middle o' de air,
  My Lord's a-writin' all de time.
He's callin' sinners from ev'rywhere.
  My Lord's a-writin' all de time.

Oh, he sees all you do
An' he hears all you say,
  My Lord's a-writin' all de time.

Come down, come down, my Lord, come down.
  My Lord's a-writin' all de time.
An' take me up to wear de crown,
  My Lord's a-writin' all de time.

Oh, he sees all you do
An' he hears all you say,
  My Lord's a-writin' all de time.

Oh, he sees all you do
An' he hears all you say,
  My Lord's a-writin' all de time.

The stage is darkened. The singing continues until the lights go up on the next scene.]

SCENE II

The tableau curtains frame the opening of a cave, which is dimly lighted. A large turkey-berry bush is somewhere near the foreground. MOSES *is seated on the grass eating his lunch from a basket in his lap.* ZIPPORAH, *his wife, stands watching him. He is about forty,* ZIPPORAH *somewhat younger. They are dressed inconspicuously. Moses stutters slightly when he speaks. He looks up to see* ZIPPORAH *smiling.*

MOSES: What you smilin' at, Zipporah?

ZIPPORAH: Caize you enjoyin' yo'self.

MOSES: You is a good wife, Zipporah.

ZIPPORAH: You is a good husband, Moses. [MOSES *wipes his mouth with a handkerchief and begins putting into the basket the various implements of the meal which had been on the ground about him.*] Why you suppose it's so dark yere today? Dey's no rain in de air.

MOSES: Seems like it's jest aroun' dis cave. Yo' father's house is got de sun on it. [*He looks in another direction.*] Looks all clear down toward Egypt.

ZIPPORAH: Co'se it *would* be fine weather in Egypt. De sky looks all right. Maybe it's gonter rain jest right yere. Why don't you move de sheep over to de other pasture?

89

MOSES: [*A bit puzzled.*] I don' know. It got dark like dis befo' you come along wid de dinner an' I was gonter stop you on de top of de hill. Den somethin' kep' me yere.

ZIPPORAH: S'pose it could be de Lawd warnin' you dat dey's 'Gyptians hangin' 'roun'?

MOSES: Dey may have fo'gotten all about dat killin' by now. Dey got a new Pharaoh down dere.

ZIPPORAH: An' I hear he's jest as mean to yo' people as his pappy was. I wouldn't put it pas' him to send soljahs all the way up yere fo' you.

MOSES: Dat's all right. De Lawd's looked after me so far, I don't 'spect him to fall down on me now. You better be gittin' home.

ZIPPORAH: [*Taking the basket.*] I'll be worryin' about you.

MOSES: [*Kissing her and then smiling.*] 'Parently de Lawd ain't. He knows I'm safe as kin be. Lemme see you feel dat way.

ZIPPORAH: You is a good man, Moses.

MOSES: I's a lucky man. [ZIPPORAH *exits with the basket.* MOSES *looks up at the sky.*] Dat's funny. De sun seems to be shinin' everyplace but right yere. It's shinin' on de sheep. Why ain't dey no cloud dere?

GOD: [*Off stage.*] Caize I want it to be like dat, Moses.

MOSES: [*Looking about him.*] Who's dat?

GOD: [*Off stage again.*] I'm de Lawd, Moses.

MOSES: [*Smiling.*] Dat's what you say. Dis yere shadow may be de Lawd's wukk, but dat voice soun' pretty much to me like my ol' brother Aaron.

GOD: [*Off stage.*] Den keep yo' eyes open, son. [*The turkey-berry bush begins to glow and then turns completely red.* MOSES *looks at it fascinated.*] Maybe you notice de bush ain't burnin' up.

MOSES: Dat's de truth. [MOSES *is full of awe but not frightened.*]

GOD: [*Off stage.*] Now you believe me?

MOSES: Co'se I does. It's wonderful. [*The light in the bush dies and* GOD *appears from behind it.*]

90

GOD: No, it ain't, Moses. It was jest a trick.

MOSES: 'Scuse me doubtin' you, Lawd. I always had de feelin' you wuz takin' keer of me, but I never 'spected you'd fin' de time to talk wid me pussunly. [*He laughs.*] Dat was a good trick, Lawd. I'se seen some good ones, but dat was de beatenest.

GOD: Yo' gonter see lots bigger tricks dan dat, Moses. In fac', yo' gonter perfo'm dem.

MOSES: [*Incredulously.*] Me? I'm gonter be a tricker?

GOD: Yes, suh.

MOSES: An' do magic? Lawd, my mouth ain't got de quick talk to go wid it.

GOD: It'll come to you now.

MOSES: [*Now cured of stuttering.*] Is I goin' wid a circus?

GOD: [*Slowly and solemnly.*] Yo' is goin' down into Egypt, Moses, and lead my people out of bondage. To do dat I'm gonter make you de bes' tricker in de worl'.

MOSES: [*A little frightened.*] Egypt! You know I killed a man dere, Lawd. Won't dey kill me?

GOD: Not when dey see yo' tricks. You ain't skeered, is you?

MOSES: [*Simply and bravely.*] No, suh, Lawd.

GOD: Den yere's what I'm gonter do. Yo' people is my chillun, Moses. I'm sick and tired o' de way ol' King Pharaoh is treatin' dem, so I'se gonter take dem away, and yo' gonter lead dem. You gonter lead 'em out of Egypt an' across de river Jordan. It's gonter take a long time, and you ain't goin' on no excursion train. Yo' gonter wukk awful hard for somethin' yo' goin' to fin' when de trip's over.

MOSES: What's dat, Lawd?

GOD: It's de Land of Canaan. It's de bes' land I got. I've promised it to yo' people, an' I'm gonter give it to dem.

MOSES: Co'se, ol' King Pharaoh will do everything he kin to stop it.

GOD: Yes, an' dat's where de tricks come in. Dey tell me he's awful fond of tricks.

93

MOSES: I hear dat's *all* he's fon' of. Dey say if you can't take a rabbit out of a hat you cain't even git in to see him.

GOD: Wait'll you see de tricks you an' me's goin' to show him.

MOSES: [*Delightedly.*] Doggone! Huh, Lawd?

GOD: Yes, suh. Now de first trick—[GOD *is lifting a stick which he carries.*]

MOSES: Jest a minute, Lawd. [GOD *halts the demonstration.*] I'm gonter learn de tricks and do just like you tell me, but I *know* it's gonter take me a little time to learn all dat quick talkin'. Cain't I have my brother Aaron go wid me? He's a good man.

GOD: I was gonter have him help you wid de Exodus. I guess he can watch, too.

MOSES: I'll call 'im. [*He turns as if to shout.*]

GOD: Wait. [MOSES *turns and looks at* GOD.] I'll *bring* him. [*Softly.*] Aaron! [AARON *appears between* GOD *and* MOSES *in the mouth of the cave. He is a little taller than* MOSES *and slightly older. He, too, is dressed like a field hand.*]

AARON: [*Blankly.*] Hey! [MOSES *goes to him, takes his hand and leads him, bewildered, down to where* MOSES *had been standing alone.* AARON *then sees* GOD.]

MOSES: [*Almost in a whisper.*] It's all right.

GOD: Don't worry, son, I'm jest showin' some tricks. Bringin' you yere was one of dem. [AARON *stares at* GOD *as if hypnotized.*] Now den, you see dis yere rod? Looks like a ordinary walking stick, don' it?

MOSES: Yes, Lawd.

GOD: Well, it ain't no ordinary walkin' stick, caize look. [MOSES *leans forward.*] When I lays it down on de groun'—[*The stage is darkened.* *The* CHOIR *begins, "Go Down, Moses,"*

When Israel was in Egyp' lan',
    Let my people go!
Oppressed so hard dey could not stan',
    Let my people go!

94

Go down, Moses, way down in Egyp' lan'
Tell ol' Pharaoh, to let my people go!

"Thus saith the Lord," bold Moses said,
    "'Let my people go!
If not I smite yo' first-born dead.
    Let my people go!'"

Go down, Moses, way down in Egyp' lan'
Tell ol' Pharaoh, to let my people go!

Go down, Moses, way down in Egyp' lan'
Tell ol' Pharaoh, to let my people go!

and continues until the lights go up on the next scene.]

SCENE III

The throne room of PHARAOH. *It suggests a Negro lodge room. The plain board walls are colored by several large parade banners of varying sizes, colors and materials, bordered with gold fringe and tassels on them. Some of the inscriptions on them read:*

SUBLIME ORDER OF PRINCES OF THE HOUSE OF PHARAOH
HOME CHAPTER

MYSTIC BROTHERS OF THE EGYPTIAN HOME GUARD
LADIES' AUXILIARY NO. I

SUPREME MAGICIANS AND WIZARDS OF THE UNIVERSE

PRIVATE FLAG OF HIS HONOR OLD KING PHARAOH

ROYAL YOUNG PEOPLE'S PLEASURE CLUB

ENCHANTED AND INVISIBLE CADETS OF EGYPT BOYS' BRIGADE

97

There is one door up right and a window. The throne, an ordinary armchair with a drapery over its back, is on a dais. PHARAOH *is seated on the throne. His crown and garments might be those worn by a high officer in a Negro lodge during a ritual. About the throne itself are high officials, several of them with plumed hats, clothing that suggests military uniforms, and rather elaborate sword belts, swords and scabbards. A few soldiers carrying spears are also in his neighborhood and one or two bearded ancients in brightly colored robes with the word "Wizard" on their conical hats. In the general group of men and women scattered elsewhere in the room Sunday finery is noticeable everywhere. Most of the civilians have bright "parade" ribbons and wear medals. In a cleared space immediately before the throne a* CANDIDATE MAGICIAN *is performing a sleight-of-hand trick with cards.* PHARAOH *watches him apathetically. He is receiving earnest attention from a few of the others, but the majority of the men and women are talking quietly among themselves. Beside the* CANDIDATE MAGICIAN *are several paraphernalia of previously demonstrated tricks.*

CANDIDATE MAGICIAN: [*Holding up some cards.*] Now, den, ol' King Pharaoh, watch dis. [*He completes a trick. There is a murmur of "Not bad." "Pretty good," etc. from a few of the watchers.* PHARAOH *makes no comment.*] Now, I believe de cyard I ast you to keep sittin' on was de trey of diamonds, wasn't it?

PHARAOH: Yeah.

CANDIDATE MAGICIAN: Den kin I trouble you to take a look at it now? [PHARAOH *half rises to pick up a card he has been sitting on, and looks at it.*] I believe you'll now notice dat it's de King of Clubs? [PHARAOH *nods and shows the card to those nearest him. The* CANDIDATE MAGICIAN *waits for an audible approval and gets practically none.*] An' dat, ol' King Pharaoh, completes de puffohmance. [*An elderly man in a uniform steps forward.*]

GENERAL: On behalf of my nephew I beg Yo' Honor to let him jine de ranks of de royal trickers and magicians.

PHARAOH: [*To the two* WIZARDS.] What do de committee think? [*The* WIZARDS *shake their heads.*] Dat's what I thought. He ain't good enough. I'd like to help you out, General, but you know a man's got to be a awful good

98

tricker to git in de royal society dese days. You better go back an' steddy some mo', son. [*He lifts his voice and directs two soldiers guarding the door.*] Is de head magician reached de royal waitin' room yit? [*One of the soldiers opens the door to look out.*] If he is, send him in. [*The soldier beckons to some one off stage, throws the door open, and announces to the court.*]

SOLDIER: De Head Magician of de land of Egypt. [*A very old and villainous man enters, his costume covered with cabalistic and zodiacal signs. He advances to the King, the other magician and his uncle making way. He bows curtly to* PHARAOH.]

HEAD MAGICIAN: Good mo'nin', ol' King Pharaoh.

PHARAOH: Mo'nin', Professor. What's de news?

HEAD MAGICIAN: Evahthing's bein' carried out like you said.

PHARAOH: How's de killin' of de babies 'mongst de Hebrews comin' 'long?

HEAD MAGICIAN: Jes' like you ordered.

PHARAOH: [*Genially.*] Dey killed all of 'em, huh?

HEAD MAGICIAN: Do dey see one, dey kill 'im. You teachin' 'em a great lesson. Dey don' like it a-tall.

PHARAOH: [*Smiling.*] What do dey say?

HEAD MAGICIAN: [*Pawing the air inarticulately.*] I hates to tell in front of de ladies.

PHARAOH: Dey feels pretty bad, huh?

HEAD MAGICIAN: Dat's jest de beginnin' of it. Betwixt de poleece and de soljahs we killed about a thousan' of 'em las' night. Dat's purty good.

PHARAOH: [*Thoughtfully.*] Yeh, it's fair. I guess you boys is doin' all you kin. But I fin' I ain't satisfied, though.

HEAD MAGICIAN: How you mean, Yo' Honor?

PHARAOH: I mean I'd like to make dose Hebrew chillun realize dat I kin be even mo' of a pest. I mean I hates dem chillun. An' I'm gonter think of a way of makin' 'em even mo' mizzable.

HEAD MAGICIAN: But dey *ain't* anythin' meaner dan killin' de babies, King.

PHARAOH: Dey must be sump'n. Doggone, you is my head tricker, you put yo' brains on it. [*To the others.*] Quiet, whilst de Head Magician go into de silence.

HEAD MAGICIAN: [*After turning completely around twice, and a moment's cogitation.*]   I tell you what I kin do. All de Hebrews dat ain't out to de buryin' grounds or in de hospitals is laborin' in de brick wukks.

PHARAOH: Yeh?

HEAD MAGICIAN: [*After a cackling laugh.*] How would it be to take de straw away from 'em and tell 'em dey's got to turn out jest as many bricks as usual? Ain't dat nasty?

PHARAOH: Purty triflin', but I s'pose it'll have to do for de time bein'. Where's de extreme inner guard? [*One of the military attendants comes forward.*] Go on out an' tell de sup'intendent to put dat into ee-ffect. [*The attendant bows and starts for the door. He stops as* PHARAOH *calls to him.*] Wait a minute! Tell 'im to chop off de hands of anybody dat say he cain't make de bricks dat way. [*The attendant salutes and exits, the door being opened and closed by one of the soldiers.*] Now what's de news in de magic line?

HEAD MAGICIAN: I ain't got very many novelties today, King, I bin wukkin' too hard on de killin's. I'm so tired I don' believe I could lift a wand. [*There are murmurs of protest from the assemblage.*]

PHARAOH: Doggone, you was to 'a been de chief feature o' de meetin' dis mawnin'. Look at de turn-out you got account of me tellin' 'em you was comin'.

HEAD MAGICIAN: Well, dat's de way it is, King. Why don' you git de wizards to do some spell castin'?

PHARAOH: Dey say it's in de cyards dat dey cain't wukk till high noon. [*He glances at the* WIZARDS.] Think mebbe you kin cheat a little?

FIRST WIZARD: Oh, dat cain't be done, King.

PHARAOH: Well, we might as well adjourn, den. Looks to me like de whole program's shot to pieces. [*He starts to rise, when there is a furious banging on the door.*]

100

What's de idea, dere? See who dat is. [*The soldiers open the door.* MOSES *and* AARON *enter, pushing the two soldiers aside and coming down in front of* PHARAOH. *The soldiers are bewildered and* PHARAOH *is angry.*] Say, who tol' you two baboons you could come in yere?

MOSES: Is you ol' King Pharaoh?

PHARAOH: Dat's me. Did you heah what I asked you?

MOSES: My name is Moses, and dis is my brother Aaron. [*Murmur of "Hebrews" spreads through the room.*]

PHARAOH: [*In a rage.*] Is you Hebrews?

MOSES: Yes, suh.

PHARAOH: [*Almost screaming.*] Put 'em to de sword! [*As the courtiers approach,* AARON *suddenly discloses the rod, which he swings once over his head. The courtiers draw back as if their hands had been stung. Cries of "Hey!" "Lookout," etc.*]

MOSES: Keep outside dat circle. [*The courtiers nearest* MOSES *and* AARON *look at each other, exclaiming ad lib., "Did you feel dat?" "What is dat?" "What's goin' on, heah?" "My hands is stingin'!" etc.*]

PHARAOH: [*Puzzled but threatening.*] What's de idea yere?

MOSES: We is magicians, ol' King Pharaoh.

PHARAOH: [*To the* HEAD MAGICIAN.] Put a spell on 'em. [*The* HEAD MAGICIAN *stands looking at them bewildered. To* MOSES.] I got some magicians, too. We'll see who's got de bes' magic. [MOSES *and* AARON *laugh. Most of the courtiers are cowering. To the* HEAD MAGICIAN.] Go ahead, give 'em gri-gri.

MOSES: Sure, go ahead.

PHARAOH: Hurry up, dey's laughin' at you. What's de matter?

HEAD MAGICIAN: I cain't think of de right spell.

PHARAOH: [*Now frightened himself.*] You mean dey got even *you* whupped?

HEAD MAGICIAN: Dey's got a new kind of magic.

PHARAOH: [*Gazes at* HEAD MAGICIAN *a moment, bewildered. To the* WIZARDS.] I s'pose if de Professor cain't, you cain't.

FIRST WIZARD: Dat's a new trick, King.

HEAD MAGICIAN: [*Rubbing his fingers along his palms.*] It's got 'lectricity in it!

PHARAOH: Hm, well dat may make it a little diff'rent. So you boys is magicians, too?

MOSES: Yes, suh.

PHARAOH: Well, we's always glad to see some new trickers in de co't, dat is if dey good. [*He glances about him.*] You look like you is O. K.

MOSES: Dat's what we claims, ol' King Pharaoh. We think we's de best in de worl'.

PHARAOH: You certainly kin talk big. Jest what is it you boys would like?

MOSES: We came to show you some tricks. Den we's goin' to ask you to do somethin' for us.

PHARAOH: Well, I s'pose you know I'm a fool for conjurin'. If a man kin show me some tricks I ain't seen, I goes out of my way to do him a favor.

MOSES: Dat's good. Want to see de first trick?

PHARAOH: It ain't goin' to hurt nobody?

MOSES: Dis one won't.

PHARAOH: Go ahead.

MOSES: Dis yere rod my brother has looks jes' like a walkin' stick, don't it? [*The courtiers now join the King in interest.*]

PHARAOH: Uh huh. Le's see. [AARON *hands him the rod, which* PHARAOH *inspects and returns.*]

MOSES: Well, look what happens when he lays it on de groun'. [AARON *places the rod on the second step of the throne. It turns into a lifelike snake. There are exclamations from the assemblage.*]

PHARAOH: Dat's a good trick! Now turn it back into a walkin' stick again. [AARON *picks it up and it is again a rod. Exclamations of "Purty good!" "Dat's all right!" "What do you think of that!" etc.*] Say, you is good trickers!

MOSES: You ain't never seen de beat of us. Now I'm goin' to ask de favor.

PHARAOH: Sure, what is it?

MOSES: [*Solemnly.*] Let de Hebrew chillun go!

PHARAOH: [*Rises and stares at them. There is a murmur of "Listen to 'im!" "He's got nerve!" "I never in my life!" "My goodness!" etc.*] What did you say?

MOSES: Let de Hebrew chillun go. [PHARAOH *seats himself again.*]

PHARAOH: [*Slowly.*] Don' you know de Hebrews is my slaves?

MOSES: Yes, suh.

PHARAOH: Yes, suh, my slaves. [*There is a distant groaning.*] Listen, and you kin hear 'em bein' treated like slaves. [*He calls toward the window.*] What was dey doin' den?

MAN NEAR THE WINDOW: Dey's jest gettin' de news down in de brick-yard.

PHARAOH: I won't let them go. [*He snorts contemptuously.*] Let's see another trick.

MOSES: Yes, suh, yere's a better one. [*He lowers his head.*] Let's have a plague of de flies. [AARON *raises the rod. The room grows dark and a great buzzing of flies is heard. The courtiers break out in cries of "Get away fum me!" "Take 'em away!" "De place is filled with flies!" "Dis is terrible!" "Do sump'n, Pharaoh!"*]

PHARAOH: [*Topping the others.*] All right—stop de trick!

MOSES: Will you let de Hebrews go?

PHARAOH: Sho' I will. Go ahead stop it!

MOSES: [*Also above the others.*] Begone! [*The buzzing stops and the room is filled with light again, as* AARON *lowers the rod. All except* MOSES *and* AARON *are brushing the flies from their persons.*]

PHARAOH: [*Laughing.*] Doggone, dat was a good trick! [*The others, seeing they are uninjured, join in the laughter, with exclamations of "Doggone!" "You all right?" "Sho' I'm all right." "Didn' hurt me." etc.*] You *is* good trickers.

MOSES: Will you let de Hebrew chillun go?

PHARAOH: [*Sitting down again.*] Well, I'll tell you, boys. I'll tell you sump'n you didn' know. You take me, *I'm* a pretty good tricker, an' I jest outtricked you. So, bein' de bes' tricker, I don' think I will let 'em go. You got any mo' tricks yo'self?

MOSES: Yes, suh. Dis is a little harder one. [AARON *lifts the rod.*] Gnats in de mill pon', gnats in de clover, gnats in de tater patch, stingin' all over. [*The stage grows dark again. There is the humming of gnats and the slapping of hands against faces and arms, and the same protests as were heard with the flies, but with more feeling, "I'm gittin' stung to death!" "I'm all stung!" "Dey're like hornets!" "Dey's on my face!" etc.*]

PHARAOH: Take 'em away, Moses!

MOSES: [*His voice drowning the others.*] If I do, will you let 'em go?

PHARAOH: Sho' I will, dis time.

MOSES: Do you mean it?

PHARAOH: Co'se I mean it! Doggone, one just stang me on de nose.

MOSES: Begone! [*Lights come up as* AARON *lowers the rod. There is a moment of general recovery again.* PHARAOH *rubs his nose, looks at his hands, etc., as do the others.*] Now, how about it?

PHARAOH: [*Smiling.*] Well, I'll tell you, Moses. Now dat de trick's over— [MOSES *takes a step toward* PHARAOH.]

MOSES: Listen, Pharaoh. You been lyin' to me, and I'm gittin' tired of it.

PHARAOH: I ain't lyin', I'm trickin', too. You been trickin' me and I been trickin' you.

MOSES: I see. Well, I got one mo' trick up my sleeve which I didn't aim to wukk unless I had to. Caize when I does it, I cain't undo it.

PHARAOH: Wukk it an' I'll trick you right back. I don' say you ain't a good tricker, Moses. You is one of de best I ever seen. But I kin outtrick you. Dat's all.

MOSES: It ain't only me dat's goin' to wukk dis trick. It's me an' de Lawd.

PHARAOH: Who?

MOSES: De Lawd God of Israel.

PHARAOH: I kin outtrick you an' de Lawd too!

MOSES: [*Angrily.*] Now you done it, ol' King Pharaoh. You been mean to de Lawd's people, and de Lawd's been easy on you caize you didn' know no better. You been givin' me a lot of say-so and no do-so, and I didn' min' dat. But now you've got to braggin' dat you's better dan de Lawd, and dat's too many.

PHARAOH: You talk like a preacher, an' I never did like to hear preachers talk.

MOSES: You ain't goin' to like it any better, when I strikes down de oldes' boy in every one of yo' people's houses.

PHARAOH: Now you've given up trickin' and is jest lyin'. [*He rises.*] Listen, I'm Pharaoh. I do de strikin' down yere. I strike down my enemies, and dere's no one in all Egypt kin kill who he wants to, 'ceptin' me.

MOSES: I'm sorry, Pharaoh. Will you let de Hebrews go?

PHARAOH: You heard my word. [AARON *is lifting his rod again at a signal from* MOSES.] Now, no more tricks or I'll—

MOSES: Oh, Lawd, you'll have to do it, I guess. Aaron, lift de rod. [*There is a thunderclap, darkness and screams. The lights go up. Several of the younger men on the stage have fallen to the ground or are being held in the arms of the horrified elders.*]

PHARAOH: What have you done yere? Where's my boy? [*Through the door come four men bearing a young man's body.*]

FIRST OF THE FOUR MEN: King Pharaoh. [PHARAOH *drops into his chair, stunned, as the dead boy is brought to the throne.*]

PHARAOH: [*Grief-stricken.*] Oh, my son, my fine son. [*The courtiers look at him with mute appeal.*]

MOSES: I'm sorry, Pharaoh, but you cain't fight de Lawd. Will you let his people go?

PHARAOH: Let them go. [*The lights go out. The* CHOIR *begins, "Oh, Mary, Don't You Weep,"*

Oh, Mary, don't you weep, don't you moan,
    Oh, Mary, don't you weep, don't you moan,
Pharaoh's army got drownded
Oh, Mary, don't you weep.

Oh, Mary, don't you weep, don't you moan,
    Oh, Mary, don't you weep, don't you moan,
Pharaoh's army got drownded
Oh, Mary, don't you weep.

Some o' dese mornin's 'bout nine o'clock
Dis ol' worl's a-gonter reel an' rock.
Pharaoh's army got drownded
Oh, Mary, don't you weep.

Oh, Mary, don't you weep, don't you moan,
    Oh, Mary, don't you weep, don't you moan,
Pharaoh's army got drownded
Oh, Mary, don't you weep.

Some o' dese mornin's bright an' fair
Take my wings an' cleave de air,
Pharaoh's army got drownded
Oh, Mary, don't you weep.

When I get to Heav'n gonter sing an' shout
Nobody dere fer ter turn me out,
Pharaoh's army got drownded
Oh, Mary, don't you weep.

When I get to Heav'n goin' to put on my shoes
Run about glory an' tell de news.
Pharaoh's army got drownded
Oh, Mary, don't you weep.

Oh, Mary, don't you weep, don't you moan,
    Oh, Mary, don't you weep, don't you moan,
Pharaoh's army got drownded
Oh, Mary, don't you weep.

Oh, Mary, don't you weep, don't you moan,
    Oh, Mary, don't you weep, don't you moan,
Pharaoh's army got drownded
Oh, Mary, don't you weep.

and continues until it is broken by the strains of "Lord, I Don' Feel No-ways Tired."

Lord, I don't feel no-ways tired
Childern, oh, glory Hallelujah!
For I hope to shout glory
When dis worl' is on fire,
Childern, oh, glory hallelujah!

The latter is sung by many more voices than the former, and the cacophony ends as the latter grows in volume and the lights go up on the next scene.]

SCENE IV

The CHILDREN OF ISRAEL *are marching on the treadmill and now singing fortissimo. They are of all ages and most of them are ragged. The men have packs on their shoulders, one or two have hand carts. The line stretches across the stage. It is nearing twilight, and the faces of the assemblage are illumined by the rays of the late afternoon sun. The upper treadmill carries a gradually rising and falling middle distance past the marchers. The foot of a mountain appears; a trumpet call is heard as the foot of the mountain reaches stage center. The marchers halt. The picture now shows the mountain running up out of sight off right. The singing stops. A babel of "What's de matter?" "Why do we stop?" "Tain't sundown yet!" "What's happened?" "What's goin' on?" "What are they blowin' for?" etc. Those looking ahead begin to murmur. "It's Moses," "Moses." "What's happened to him?" The others take up the repetition of "Moses," and* MOSES *enters, on the arm of* AARON. *He is now an old man, as is his brother, and he totters toward the center of the stage. Cries of "What's de matter, Moses?" "You ain't hurt, is you?" "Ain't that too bad?" etc. He slowly seats himself on the rock at the foot of the mountain.*

AARON: How you feelin' now, brother?

MOSES: I'm so weary, Aaron. Seems like I was took all of a sudden.

AARON: Do we camp yere?

MOSES: [*Pathetically.*] No, you got to keep goin'.

AARON: But you cain't go no further tonight, brother.

MOSES: Dis never happened to me befo'.

A YOUNG WOMAN: But you's a ol' man, now, Father Moses. You cain't expect to go as fas' as we kin.

MOSES: But de Lawd said I'd do it. He said I was to show you de Promised Land. Fo'ty years, I bin leadin' you. I led you out o' Egypt. I led you past Sinai, and through de wilderness. Oh, I cain't fall down on you now!

AARON: Le's res' yere fo' de night. Den we'll see how you feel in de mo'nin'.

MOSES: We tol' de scouts we'd meet 'em three miles furder on. I hate fo' 'em to come back all dis way to report. 'Tis gettin' a little dark, ain't it?

AARON: It ain't dark, Brother.

MOSES: No, it's my eyes.

AARON: Maybe it's de dust.

MOSES: No, I jest cain't seem to see. Oh, Lawd, dey cain't have a blind man leadin' 'em! Where is you, Aaron?

AARON: I'se right yere, Moses.

MOSES: Do you think—[*Pause.*] Oh! Do you think it's de time He said?

AARON: How you mean, Moses? [*Crowd look from one to another in wonder.*]

MOSES: He said I could lead 'em to de Jordan, dat I'd *see* de Promised Land, and dat's all de further I could go, on account I broke de laws. Little while back I thought *I did* see a river ahead, and a pretty land on de other side. [*Distant shouts "Hooray!" "Yere dey are!" "Dey travelled quick." etc.*] Where's de young leader of de troops? Where's Joshua? [*The call "Joshua" is taken up by those on the right of the stage, followed almost immediately by "Yere he is!" "Moses wants you!" etc.* JOSHUA *enters. He is a fine looking Negro of about thirty.*]

JOSHUA: [*Going to* MOSES' *side.*] Yes, suh.

MOSES: What's de shoutin' 'bout, Joshua?

JOSHUA: De scouts is back wid de news. De Jordan is right ahead of us,

and Jericho is jest on de other side. Moses, we're dere! [*There are cries of "Hallelujah!" "De Lawd be praised!" "Hooray!" "De Kingdom's comin'!" etc. With a considerable stir among the marchers, several new arrivals crowd in from right, shouting "Moses, we're dere!"* JOSHUA *seeing the newcomers.*] Yere's de scouts! [*Three very ragged and dusty young men advance to* MOSES.]

MOSES: [*As the shouting dies.*] So it's de River Jordan?

FIRST SCOUT: Yes, suh.

MOSES: All we got to take is de city of Jericho.

FIRST SCOUT: Yes, suh.

MOSES: Joshua, you got to take charge of de fightin' men, an' Aaron's gotta stay by de priests.

JOSHUA: What about you?

MOSES: You are leavin' me behind. Joshua, you gonter get de fightin' men together and take dat city befo' sundown.

JOSHUA: It's a big city, Moses, wid walls all 'round it. We ain't got enough men.

MOSES: You'll take it, Joshua.

JOSHUA: Yes, suh, but how?

MOSES: Move up to de walls wid our people. Tell de priests to go wid you with de rams' horns. You start marchin' 'roun' dem walls, and den—

JOSHUA: Yes, suh.

MOSES: De Lawd'll take charge, jest as he's took charge ev'y time I've led you against a city. He ain't never failed, has he?

SEVERAL VOICES: No, Moses. [*All raise their heads.*]

MOSES: And he ain't goin' to fail us now. [*He prays. All bow.*] Oh, Lawd, I'm turnin' over our brave young men to you, caize I know you don' want me to lead 'em any further. [*Rises.*] Jest like you said, I've got to de Jordan but I cain't git over it. An' yere dey goin' now to take de city of Jericho. In a little while dey'll be marchin' 'roun' it. An' would you please be so good as to tell 'em what to do? Amen. [*To* JOSHUA.] Go ahead. Ev'ybody follows Joshua now. Give de signal to move on wid e'vything. [*A trumpet is heard.*] You camp fo' de night in de City of Jericho. [MOSES *seats himself on the rock.*]

JOSHUA: Cain't we help you, Moses?

MOSES: You go ahead. De Lawd's got his plans fo' me. Soun' de signal to march. [*Another trumpet call is heard. The company starts marching off.* AARON *lingers a moment.*] Take care of de Ark of de Covenant, Aaron.

AARON: Yes, Brother. Good-bye.

MOSES: Good-bye, Aaron. [*The singing is resumed, then dies away as the last of the marchers disappears.*] Yere I is, Lawd. De chillun is goin' into de Promised Land. [GOD *enters from behind the hill. He walks to* MOSES, *puts his hands on his shoulders.*] You's with me, ain't you, Lawd?

GOD: Co'se I is.

MOSES: Guess I'm through, Lawd. Jest like you said I'd be, when I broke de tablets of de law. De ol' machine's broke down.

GOD: Jest what was it I said to you, Moses? Do you remember?

MOSES: You said I couldn't go into de Promised Land.

GOD: Dat's so. But dat ain't all dey was to it.

MOSES: How you mean, Lawd?

GOD: Moses, you been a good man. You been a good leader of my people. You got me angry once, dat's true. And when you anger me I'm a God of Wrath. But I never meant you wasn't gonter have what was comin' to you. An' I ain't goin' to do you out of it, Moses. It's jest de country acrost de River dat you ain't gonter enter. You gonter have a Promised Land. I been gettin' it ready fo' you, fo' a long time. Kin you stand up?

MOSES: [*Rising, with* GOD's *help.*] Yes, suh, Lawd.

GOD: Come on, I'm goin' to show it to you. We goin' up dis hill to see it. Moses, it's a million times nicer dan de Land of Canaan. [*They start up the hill.*]

MOSES: I cain't hardly see.

GOD: Don't worry. Dat's jest caize you so old. [*They take a step or two up the hill, when* MOSES *stops suddenly.*]

114

MOSES: Oh!

GOD: What's de matter?

MOSES: We cain't be doin' dis!

GOD: Co'se we kin!

MOSES: But I fo'got! I fo'got about Joshua and de fightin' men!

GOD: How about 'em?

MOSES: Dey're marchin' on Jericho. I tol' 'em to march aroun' de walls and den de Lawd would be dere to tell 'em what to do.

GOD: Dat's all right. He's dere.

MOSES: Den who's dis helpin' me up de hill?

GOD: Yo' faith, yo' God.

MOSES: And is you over dere helpin' them too, Lawd? Is you goin' to tell dem poor chillun what to do?

GOD: Co'se I is. Listen, Moses. I'll show you how I'm helpin' dem. [*From the distance comes the blast of the rams' horns, the sound of crumbling walls, a roar, and a moment's silence. The* CHOIR *begins "Joshua Fit De Battle of Jericho"*

Joshua fit de battle of Jericho, Jericho, Jericho
Joshua fit de battle of Jericho,
An' de walls come tumblin' down.

Joshua fit de battle of Jericho, Jericho, Jericho
Joshua fit de battle of Jericho,
An' de walls come tumblin' down.

Up to de walls of Jericho
He marched wid spear in han'
"Go blow dem ram-horns," Joshua cried,
"Kase de battle am in my han'."

Dat mornin', Joshua fit de battle of Jericho, Jericho, Jericho
Joshua fit de battle of Jericho,
An' de walls come tumblin' down.

and continues through the rest of the scene.]

MOSES: You did it, Lawd! You've tooken it! Listen to de chillun—dey's in de Land of Canaan at last! You's de only God dey ever was, ain't you, Lawd?

GOD: [*Quietly.*] Come on, ol' man. [*They continue up the hill. The stage is darkened.*]

MR. DESHEE: [*In the dark.*] But even dat scheme didn' work. Caize after dey got into de Land of Canaan dey went to de dogs again. And dey went into bondage again. Only dis time it was in de City of Babylon. [*The* CHOIR, *which has been singing "Lord, I Can't Stay Away,"*

Lord, I can't stay away,
I can't stay away,
Lord, I can't stay away,
    I wish I had died in de Egyp' lan'.

Lord, I can't stay away,
I can't stay away,
Lord, I can't stay away,
    I wish I had died in de Egyp' lan'.

Children grumbled on de way,
    I wish I had died in de Egyp' lan'
Children dey forgot to pray,
    I wish I had died in de Egyp' lan'.

116

Lord, I can't stay away,
I can't stay away,
Lord, I can't stay away,
    I wish I had died in de Egyp' lan'.

Lord, I can't stay away,
I can't stay away,
Lord, I can't stay away,
    I wish I had died in de Egyp' lan'.

stops as the next scene begins.]

SCENE V

Under a low ceiling is a room vaguely resembling a Negro night club in New Orleans. Two or three long tables run across the room, and on the left is a table on a dais with a gaudy canopy above it. The table bears a card marked "Reserved for King and guests." Flashy young men and women are seated at the tables. About a dozen couples are dancing in the foreground to the tune of a jazz orchestra. The costumes are what would be worn at a Negro masquerade to represent the debauches of Babylon.

FIRST MAN: When did yuh git to Babylon?

SECOND MAN: I jes' got in yesterday.

THIRD MAN: [*Dancing.*] How do you like dis baby, Joe?

FOURTH MAN: Hot damn! She could be de King's pet!

A WOMAN: Anybody seen my papa?

THIRD MAN: Don' fo'git de dance at de High Priest's house tomorrow.

[*The dance stops as a bugle call is heard. Enter* MASTER OF CEREMONIES.]

MASTER OF CEREMONIES: Stop! Tonight's guest of honor, de King of Babylon an' party of five. [*Enter the* KING *and five girls. The* KING *has on an imitation ermine cloak over his conventional evening clothes and wears a diamond tiara. All rise as the* KING *enters, and sing, "Hail, de King of Bab—Bab—Babylon."*[1]

---

[1] Words and music written especially by Mr. Hall Johnson for "The Green Pastures."

119

Hail de King of Bab—Bab—Babylon,
Hail de King of Bab—Bab—Babylon,
Hail de King of Bab—Bab—Babylon,
No place like Babylon.

KING: Wait till you see de swell table I got. [*He crosses the stage to his table. The girls are jabbering.*] Remind me to send you a peck of rubies in de mo'nin'.

MASTER OF CEREMONIES: Ev'nin', King!

KING: Good ev'nin'. How's de party goin'?

MASTER OF CEREMONIES: Bes' one we ever had in Babylon, King.

KING: Any Jew boys yere?

MASTER OF CEREMONIES: [*Indicating some of the others.*] Lot o' dem yere. I kin go git mo' if you want 'em.

KING: I was really referrin' to de High Priest. He's a 'ticlar frien' o' mine an' he might drop in. You know what he look like?

MASTER OF CEREMONIES: No, suh, but I'll be on de look-out fo' him.

KING: O.K. Now le's have a li'l good time.

MASTER OF CEREMONIES: Yes, suh. [*To the orchestra.*] Let 'er go, boys. [*The music begins, waiters appear with food and great urns painted gold and silver, from which they pour out wine for the guests. The* MASTER OF CEREMONIES *exits. The* KING'S *dancing-girls go to the middle of the floor, and start to dance. The* KING *puts his arms about the waists of two girls, and draws them to him.*]

KING: Hot damn! Da's de way! Let de Jew boys see our gals kin dance better'n dere's. [*There is an ad lib. babel of* "Da's de truth, King!" "I don' know— we got some good gals, too!" *etc.*] Dey ain' nobody in de worl' like de Babylon gals. [*The dancing grows faster, the watchers keep time with hand-claps. The door at the left opens suddenly, and the* PROPHET, *a patriarchal, ragged figure enters. He looks belligerently about the room, and is followed almost immediately by the* MASTER OF CEREMONIES.]

120

PROPHET: Stop! [*The music and the dancers halt.*]

KING: What's the idea, bustin' up my party?

MASTER OF CEREMONIES: He said he was expected, King. I thought mebbe he was de—

KING: Did you think he was de High Priest of de Hebrews? Why, he's jest an ol' bum! De High Priest is a fashion plate. T'row dis ole bum out o' yere!

PROPHET: Stop! [*Those who have been advancing to seize him stop, somewhat amused.*]

KING: Wait a minute. Don't throw him out. Let's see what he has to say.

PROPHET: Listen to me, King of Babylon! I've been sent yere by de Lawd God Jehovah. Don't you dare lay a hand on de Prophet!

KING: Oh, you're a prophet, is yuh? Well, you know we don' keer much fo' prophets in dis part of de country.

PROPHET: Listen to me, sons and daughters of Babylon! Listen, you children of Israel dat's given yo'selves over to de evil ways of yo' oppressors! You're all wallowin' like hogs in sin, an' de wrath of Gawd ain' goin' to be held back much longer! I'm tellin' you, repent befo' it's too late. Repent befo' Jehovah casts down de same fire dat burned up Sodom and Gomorrah. Repent befo' de—[*During this scene yells increase as the* PROPHET *continues. The* HIGH PRIEST *enters Left. He is a fat voluptuary elaborately clothed in brightly colored robes. He walks in hand in hand with a gaudily dressed "chippy."*]

HIGH PRIEST: [*Noise stops.*] Whoa, dere! What you botherin' the King fo'?

PROPHET: [*Wheeling.*] And you, de High Priest of all Israel, walkin' de town wid a dirty li'l tramp.

KING: Seems to be a frien' o' yours, Jake.

HIGH PRIEST: [*Crossing to the* KING *with his girl.*] Aw, he's one of dem wild men, like Jeremiah and Isaiah. Don' let him bother you none. [*Pushes* PROPHET *aside and goes to* KING'S *table.*]

PROPHET: You consort with harlots, an' yo' pollution in the sight of de

Lawd. De Lawd God's goin' to smite you down, jest as he's goin' to smite down all dis wicked world! [*Grabs* HIGH PRIEST *and turns him around.*]

KING: [*Angrily against the last part of the preceding speech.*] Wait a minute. I'm getting tired of this. Don' throw him out. Jest kill him! [*There is the sound of a shot. The* PROPHET *falls.*]

PROPHET: Smite 'em down, Lawd, like you said. Dey ain't a decent person left in de whole world. [*He dies.* MASTER OF CEREMONIES, *revolver in hand, looks down at the* PROPHET.]

MASTER OF CEREMONIES: He's dead, King.

KING: Some of you boys take him out. [*A couple of young men come from the background and walk off with the body.*]

HIGH PRIEST: Don' know whether you should 'a done that, King.

KING: Why not?

HIGH PRIEST: I don' know whether de Lawd would like it.

KING: Now, listen, Jake. You know yo' Lawd ain't payin' much attention to dis man's town. Except fo' you boys, it's tho'ly protected by de Gods o' Babylon.

HIGH PRIEST: I know, but jest de same—

KING: Look yere, s'pose I give you a couple hund'ed pieces of silver. Don' you s'pose you kin arrange to persuade yo' Gawd to keep his hands off?

HIGH PRIEST: [*Oilily.*] Well of co'se we could try. I dunno how well it would work. [*As the* HIGH PRIEST *speaks, the* KING *claps his hands.* MASTER OF CEREMONIES *enters with bag of money.*]

KING: Yere it is.

HIGH PRIEST: [*Smiling.*] I guess we kin square things up. [*He prays— whiningly.*] Oh Lawd, please forgive my po' frien' de King o' Babylon. He didn't know what he was doin' an'—[*There is a clap of thunder, darkness for a second. The lights go up and* GOD *is standing in the center of the room.*]

GOD: [*In a voice of doom.*] Dat's about enough. [*The guests are horrified.*] I's stood all I kin from you. I tried to make dis a good earth. I helped Adam, I

122

helped Noah, I helped Moses, an' I helped David. What's de grain dat grew out of de seed? Sin! Nothin' but sin throughout de whole world. I've given you ev'y chance. I sent you warriors and prophets. I've given you laws and commandments, an' you betrayed my trust. Ev'ything I've given you, you've defiled. Ev'y time I've forgiven you, you've mocked me. An, now de High Priest of Israel tries to trifle wid my name. Listen, you chillun of darkness, yo' Lawd is tired. I'm tired of de struggle to make you worthy of de breath I gave you. I put you in bondage ag'in to cure you an' yo' worse dan you was amongst de flesh pots of Egypt. So I renounce you. Listen to the words of yo' lawd God Jehovah, for dey is de last words yo' ever hear from me. I repent of dese people dat I have made and I will deliver dem no more.   [*There is darkness and cries of "Mercy!" "Have pity, Lawd!" "We didn' mean it, Lawd!" "Forgive us, Lawd!" etc. The* CHOIR *sings "Death's Gonter Lay His Cold Icy Han's On Me"*

> Cryin' "Oh, Lord," cryin' "Oh, my Lord,"
> Cryin' "Oh, Lord,"
>> Death's gonter lay his cold icy han's on me.
>
> Cryin' "Oh, Lord," cryin' "Oh, my Lord,"
> Cryin' "Oh, Lord,"
>> Death's gonter lay his cold icy han's on me.
>
> Oh, sinner, sinner, you better pray,
>> Death's gonter lay his cold icy han's on me.
> Or your soul git lost at de Jedgment day.
>> Death's gonter lay his cold icy han's on me.
>
> Cryin' "Oh, Lord," cryin' "Oh, my Lord,"
> Cryin' "Oh, Lord,"
>> Death's gonter lay his cold icy han's on me.

until the lights go up on the next scene.]

SCENE VI

GOD *is writing at his desk. Outside, past the door, goes* HOSEA, *a dignified old man, with wings like* JACOB'S. GOD, *sensing his presence, looks up from the paper he is examining, and follows him out of the corner of his eye. Angrily he resumes his work as soon as* HOSEA *is out of sight. There is a knock on the door.*

GOD: Who is it? [GABRIEL *enters.*]

GABRIEL: It's de delegation, Lawd.

GOD: [*Wearily.*] Tell 'em to come in. [ABRAHAM, ISAAC, JACOB, *and* MOSES *enter.*]

Good mo'nin', gen'lemen.

THE VISITORS: Good mo'nin', Lawd.

GOD: What kin I do for you?

MOSES: You know, Lawd. Go back to our people.

GOD: [*Shaking his head.*] Ev'ry day fo' hund'eds of years you boys have come in to ask dat same thing. De answer is still de same. I repented of de people I made. I said I would deliver dem no more. Good mo'nin', gen'lemen. [*The four visitors rise and exeunt.* GABRIEL *remains.*] Gabe, why do dey do it?

GABRIEL: I 'spect dey think you gonter change yo' mind.

GOD: [*Sadly.*] Dey don' know me. [HOSEA *again passes the door. His shadow shows on wall.* GABRIEL *is perplexed, as he watches.* GOD *again looks surreptitiously over His shoulder at the passing figure.*] I don' like dat, either.

GABRIEL: What, Lawd?

GOD: Dat man.

GABRIEL: He's jest a prophet, Lawd. Dat's jest old Hosea. He jest come up the other day.

GOD: I know. He's one of de few dat's come up yere since I was on de earth last time.

GABRIEL: Ain' been annoyin' you, has he?

GOD: I don' like him walkin' past de door.

GABRIEL: All you got to do is tell him to stop, Lawd.

GOD: Yes, I know. I don' want to tell him. He's got a right up yere or he wouldn' be yere.

GABRIEL: You needn' be bothered by him hangin' aroun' de office all de time. I'll tell 'im. Who's he think he—

GOD: No, Gabe. I find it ain't in me to stop him. I sometimes jest wonder why he don' come in and say hello.

GABRIEL: You want him to do dat? [*He moves as if to go to the door.*]

GOD: He never has spoke to me, and if he don' wanta come in, I ain't gonter make him. But dat ain't de worst of it, Gabriel.

GABRIEL: What is, Lawd?

GOD: Ev'y time he goes past de door I hears a voice.

GABRIEL: One of de angels?

GOD: [*Shaking his head.*] It's from de earth. It's a man.

GABRIEL: You mean he's prayin'?

GOD: No, he ain't exactly prayin'. He's jest talkin' in such a way dat I got to lissen. His name is Hezdrel.

GABRIEL: Is he on de books?

GOD: No, not yet. But ev'y time dat Hosea goes past I hear dat voice.

GABRIEL: Den tell *it* to stop.

GOD: I find I don' want to do that, either. Dey's gettin' ready to take Jerusalem down dere. Dat was my big fine city. Dis Hezdrel, he's jest one of de defenders. [*Suddenly and passionately, almost wildly.*] I ain't comin' down. You hear me? I ain't comin' down. [*He looks at* GABRIEL.] Go ahead, Gabriel. 'Tend to yo' chores. I'm gonter keep wukkin' yere.

GABRIEL: I hates to see you feelin' like dis, Lawd.

GOD: Dat's all right. Even bein' Gawd ain't no bed of roses. [GABRIEL *exits.* HOSEA'S *shadow is on the wall. For a second* HOSEA *hesitates.* GOD *looks at the wall. Goes to window.*] I hear you. I know yo' fightin' bravely, but I ain't comin' down. Oh, why don' you leave me alone? You know you ain't talkin' to me. *Is* you talkin' to me? I cain't stand yo' talkin' dat way. I kin only hear part of what you' sayin', and it puzzles me. Don' you know you cain't puzzle God. [*A pause. Then tenderly.*] Do you want me to come down dere ve'y much? You know I said I wouldn't come down? [*Fiercely.*] Why don' he answer me a little? [*With clenched fists, looks down through the window.*] Listen! I'll tell you what I'll do. I ain't goin' to promise you anythin', and I ain't goin' to do nothin' to help you. I'm jest feelin' a little low, an' I'm only comin' down to make myself feel a little better, dat's all. [*The stage is darkened.* CHOIR *begins "De Blin' Man Stood on de Road an' Cried,"*

O, de blin' man stood on de road an' cried,
O, de blin' man stood on de road an' cried,
Cryin', "Oh, Lordy, save me."
O, de blin' man stood on de road an' cried.

and continues until the lights go up on the next scene.]

SCENE VII

It is a shadowed corner beside the walls of the temple in Jerusalem. The light of camp fires flickers on the figure of HEZDREL, *who was* ADAM *in Part I. He stands in the same position* ADAM *held when first discovered but in his right hand is a sword, and his left is in a sling. Around him are several prostrate bodies. Pistol and cannon shots, then a trumpet call. Six young men enter from left in command of a* CORPORAL. *They are all armed.*

CORPORAL: De fightin's stopped fo' de night, Hezdrel.

HEZDREL: Yes?

CORPORAL: Dey're goin' to begin ag'in at cockcrow. [*Man enters, crosses the stage and exits.*]   Herod say he's goin' to take de temple tomorrow, burn de books and de Ark of de Covenant, and put us all to de sword.

HEZDREL: Yo' ready, ain't you?

EVERYBODY: Yes, Hezdrel.

HEZDREL: Did de food get in through de hole in de city wall? [*Two soldiers enter, cross the stage and exit.*]

CORPORAL: Yessuh, we's goin' back to pass it out now.

HEZDREL: Good. Any mo' of our people escape today?

CORPORAL: Ol' Herod's got de ol' hole covered up now, but fifteen of our people got out a new one we made. [*Other soldiers enter, cross the stage and exit.*]

HEZDREL: Good. Take dese yere wounded men back and git 'em took care of.

CORPORAL: Yes, suh. [*They pick up the bodies on the ground and carry them off-stage as* HEZDREL *speaks.*]

HEZDREL: So dey gonter take de temple in de mo'nin'? We'll be waitin' for 'em. Jest remember, boys, when dey kill us we leap out of our skins, right into de lap of God. [*The men disappear with the wounded; from the deep shadow upstage comes* GOD.]

GOD: Hello, Hezdrel—Adam.

HEZDREL: [*Rubbing his forehead.*] Who is you?

GOD: Me? I'm jest an ol' preacher, from back in de hills.

HEZDREL: What you doin' yere?

GOD: I heard you boys was fightin'. I jest wanted to see how it was goin'.

HEZDREL: Well, it ain't goin' so well.

GOD: Dey got you skeered, huh?

HEZDREL: Look yere, who is you, a spy in my brain?

GOD: Cain't you see I's one of yo' people?

HEZDREL: Listen, Preacher, we ain't skeered. We's gonter be killed, but we ain't skeered.

GOD: I's glad to hear dat. Kin I ask you a question, Hezdrel?

HEZDREL: What is it?

GOD: How is it you is so brave?

HEZDREL: Caize we got faith, dat's why!

GOD: Faith? In who?

HEZDREL: In our dear Lawd God.

GOD: But God say he abandoned ev' one down yere.

HEZDREL: Who say dat? Who dare say dat of the Lawd God of Hosea?

132

GOD: De God of Hosea?

HEZDREL: You heard me. Look yere, you *is* a spy in my brain!

GOD: No, I ain't, Hezdrel. I'm jest puzzled. You ought to know dat.

HEZDREL: How come you so puzzled 'bout de God of Hosea?

GOD: I don' know. Maybe I jest don' hear things. You see, I live 'way back in de hills.

HEZDREL: What you wanter find out?

GOD: Ain't de God of Hosea de same Jehovah dat was de God of Moses?

HEZDREL: [*Contemptuously.*] No. Dat ol' God of wrath and vengeance? We have de God dat Hosea preached to us. He's de one God.

GOD: Who's he?

HEZDREL: [*Reverently.*] De God of mercy.

GOD: Hezdrel, don' you think dey must be de same God?

HEZDREL: I don' know. I ain't bothered to think much about it. Maybe dey is. Maybe our God is de same ol' God. I guess we jest got tired of his appearance dat ol' way.

GOD: What you mean, Hezdrel?

HEZDREL: Oh, dat ol' God dat walked de earth in de shape of a man. I guess he lived wid man so much dat all he seen was de sins in man. Dat's what made him de God of wrath and vengeance. Co'se he made Hosea. An' Hosea never would 'a' found what mercy was unless dere was a little of it in God, too. Anyway, he ain't a fearsome God no mo'. Hosea showed us dat.

GOD: How you s'pose Hosea found dat mercy?

HEZDREL: De only way he could find it. De only way I found it. De only way anyone kin find it.

GOD: How's dat?

HEZDREL: Through sufferin'.

GOD: [*After a pause.*] What if dey kill you in de mo'nin', Hezdrel.

HEZDREL: If dey do, dey do. Dat's all.

GOD: Herod say he's goin' to burn de temple—

HEZDREL: So he say.

GOD: And burn de Ark an' de books. Den dat's de end of de books, ain't it?

HEZDREL: [*Buoyantly.*] What you mean? If he burns dem things in dere? Naw. Dem's jest copies.

GOD: Where is de others?

HEZDREL: [*Tapping his head.*] Dey's a set in yere. Fifteen got out through de hole in the city wall today. A hundred and fifty got out durin' de week. Each of em is a set of de books. Dey's scattered safe all over de countryside now, jest waitin' to git pen and paper fo' to put 'em down agin.

GOD: [*Proudly.*] Dey cain't lick you, kin dey, Hezdrel?

HEZDREL: [*Smiling.*] I know dey cain't. [*Trumpet.*] You better get out o' yere, Preacher, if you wanter carry de news to yo' people. It'll soon be daylight.

GOD: I'm goin'. [*He takes a step upstage and stops.*] Want me to take any message?

HEZDREL: Tell de people in de hills dey ain't nobody like de Lawd God of Hosea.

GOD: I will. If dey kill you tomorrow I'll bet dat God of Hosea'll be waitin' for you.

HEZDREL: I *know* he will.

GOD: [*Quietly.*] Thank you, Hezdrel.

HEZDREL: Fo' what?

GOD: Fo' tellin' me so much. You see I been so far away, I guess I was jest way behin' de times. [*He exits. Pause, then trumpet sounds.* HEZDREL *paces back and forth once or twice. Another young soldier appears. Other men enter and stand grouped about* HEZDREL.]

SECOND OFFICER: [*Excitedly.*] De cock's jest crowed, Hezdrel. Dey started de fightin' ag'in.

HEZDREL: We's ready for 'em. Come on, boys. [*From the darkness upstage comes another group of soldiers.*] Dis is de day dey say dey'll git us. Le's fight till de last man goes. What d'you say?

136

CORPORAL: Le's go, Hezdrel!

HEZDREL: [*Calling left.*] Give 'em ev'ything, boys!

[*There is a movement toward the left, a bugle call and the sound of distant battle. The lights go out. The* CHOIR *is heard singing, "March On,"*

> Way over in de Egyp' lan',
> You shall gain de victory;
> Heard good news from de promise' lan'
> You shall gain de day.
>
> March on, an' you shall gain de victory,
> So march on, an' you shall gain de day.
>
> O, Children, march on, an you shall gain de victory,
> So march on, an' you shall gain de day.

triumphantly. They continue to sing after the lights go up on the next scene.]

SCENE VIII

It is the same setting as the Fish Fry Scene in Part I. The same angels are present but the CHOIR *marches, circling on one side of the stage singing softly and slowly "Rise an' Shine."*

Oh, Rise an' shine,
    An' give God de glory, glory
Rise an' shine.
    An' give God de glory, glory
Rise an' shine.
    An' give God de glory, glory
For de year of Jubilee.

Oh, Rise an' shine,
    An' give God de glory, glory
Rise an' shine.
    An' give God de glory, glory
Rise an' shine.
    An' give God de glory, glory
For de year of Jubilee.

GOD *is seated in an armchair near center. He faces the audience. As the* CHOIR *continues to sing,* GABRIEL *enters, unnoticed by the chattering angels. He looks at* GOD *who is staring thoughtfully toward the audience.*

GABRIEL: You look a little pensive, Lawd. [GOD *nods his head.*] Have a seegar, Lawd?

GOD: No thanks, Gabriel.

[GABRIEL *goes to the table, accepts a cup of custard; chats with the angel behind the table for a moment as he sips, puts the cup down and returns to the side of* GOD.]

GABRIEL: You look awful pensive, Lawd. You been sittin' yere, lookin' dis way, an awful long time. Is it somethin' serious, Lawd?

GOD: Very serious, Gabriel.

GABRIEL: [*Awed by His tone.*] Lawd, is de time come for me to blow?

GOD: Not yet, Gabriel. I'm just thinkin'.

GABRIEL: What about, Lawd? [*Puts up hand. Singing stops.*]

GOD: 'Bout somethin' de boy tol' me. Somethin' 'bout Hosea, and himself. How dey foun' somethin'.

GABRIEL: What, Lawd?

GOD: Mercy. [*A pause.*] Through *sufferin'*, he said.

GABRIEL: Yes, Lawd.

GOD: I'm tryin' to find it, too. It's awful impo'tant. It's awful impo'tant to all de people on my earth. Did he mean dat even God must suffer?

[GOD *continues to look out over the audience for a moment and then a look of surprise comes into his face. He sighs. In the distance a voice cries.*]

THE VOICE: Oh, look at him! Oh, look, dey goin' to make him carry it up dat high hill! Dey goin' to nail him to it! Oh, dat's a terrible burden for one man to carry!

GOD *rises and murmurs "Yes!" as if in recognition. The heavenly beings have been watching him closely, and now, seeing him smile gently, draw back, relieved. All the angels burst into "Hallelujah, King Jesus."* [2]

[2]The words and music were written especially for "The Green Pastures" by Mr. Hall Johnson.

140

Hallelujah, King Jesus
Hallelujah, King Jesus,
Hallelujah, King Jesus,
God of mercy,
Lord of love!

Hallelujah, King Jesus
Hallelujah, King Jesus,
Hallelujah, King Jesus,
God of mercy,
Lord of love!

Hallelujah, King Jesus
Hallelujah, King Jesus,
Hallelujah, King Jesus,
God of mercy,
Lord of love!

God continues to smile as the lights fade away. The singing becomes fortissimo.

CURTAIN